Vegan

Soups and Hearty Stews

for All Seasons

Also by Nava Atlas

Vegan Express

The Vegetarian Family Cookbook

The Vegetarian 5-Ingredient Gourmet

Pasta East to West

Great American Vegetarian

Vegetarian Express

Vegetariana

Vegetarian Celebrations

VEGAN
SOUPS and HEARTY STEWS
for ALL SEASONS

Nava Atlas

Broadway Books
New York

BROADWAY

Published in the United States by Broadway Books,
an imprint of The Doubleday Publishing Group,
a division of Random House, Inc., New York.
www.broadwaybooks.com

Previous versions were self-published by Amberwood Press
in 1992, 1996, and 2006.

BROADWAY BOOKS and its logo,
a letter B bisected on the diagonal,
are trademarks of Random House, Inc.

Book design by Nava Atlas and Amy Papaelias
Photographs by Theresa Raffetto
Food styling by Jessica Gorman

Library of Congress Cataloging-in-Publication Data
Atlas, Nava.
    Vegan soups and hearty stews for all seasons /
written and illustrated by Nava Atlas. —4th ed.
        p. cm.
    Previously published under title: Vegetarian soups for all seasons.
    Includes index.
    1. Soups. 2. Stews. 3. Vegan cookery. I. Atlas, Nava. Vegetarian soups
for all seasons. II. Title.

    TX757.A85 2009
    641.5′636—dc22

                              2008021922

ISBN 978-0-7679-3072-7

PRINTED IN THE UNITED STATES OF AMERICA

10 9 8 7 6 5 4 3 2 1

Revised Edition

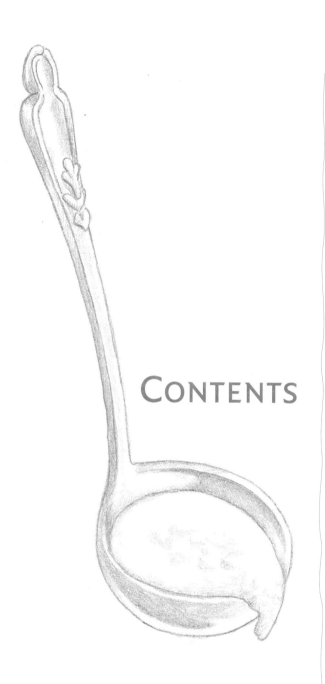

CONTENTS

INTRODUCTION AND BASICS

Soups have always held a prominent spot in my culinary repertoire, being one of the easiest, yet most rewarding, of all preparations in the kitchen. One hardly needs to go beyond the most basic of ingredients and equipment to create a wonderfully diverse range of possibilities and results: A soup might be familiar and soothing, evoking memories of the warmth and comfort of a childhood home, or it might be a mélange of sophisticated flavors that meld together in a pleasantly unexpected way. Or with a bit less liquid and a tad more chunkiness of texture, the result is stew—a savory and satisfying one-pot meal.

Soups and stews are welcome at any time of year, reflecting the harvest of each season. Good soups and stews can:

- brighten a humdrum winter day and give comfort when colds and viruses hit
- showcase the tender new produce of spring or the bounty of fall's harvest
- transform the lush diversity of summer's fruits and vegetables into refreshing elixirs

This new edition (this book's fourth) reflects the decision I made a few years ago to go vegan, following in the footsteps of my sons. My husband and I raised our sons as lacto-ovo vegetarians from birth; our youngest son, at age 10, decided to become a vegan for ethical reasons. Our older son, then not quite 13, followed suit shortly thereafter. Inspired by their conviction, it didn't take long for my husband and me to join them.

Being vegan in the 21st century is not much different from being a vegetarian. There are many substitutions for dairy products (including soy, rice, and nut-based milks, cheeses, and the like), and unless you crave omelets, it's surprisingly easy to dispense with eggs in the diet. I love to bake, and happily discovered that eggs are just not necessary to make good baked goods. This is reflected in the revised chapter of accompaniments, which includes quick breads, muffins, biscuits, and such.

Veganism is primarily about ethics—what we put on our plates reflects ideals about having compassion toward all living beings, saving the environment from the ravages of animal agriculture, and preventing diseases caused by the Western diet. But veganism is also about enjoyment of great food—vegans may have political palates, but they are also quite discerning. The many vegan restaurants that have sprung up everywhere over the last decade feature some of the most creative, delicious food anywhere, and the gourmet food industry aimed squarely at the vegan market has blossomed tremendously. This love for fantastic fare served with a clear conscience is most gratifying in one's own kitchen.

From one soup lover to another, here are scores of soups for any time of year. It almost goes without saying that you need not be a vegan—or even a vegetarian—to enjoy these recipes. Low in fat, high in fiber, and globally inspired, they are for everyone who appreciates fresh and flavorful seasonal produce, whole grains, healthful beans, legumes, and soyfoods, with the judicious use of herbs, spices, and other seasonings. Best of all is the sense of comfort and wonderful aromas imparted by a big pot of simmering soup or stew, whetting the appetite like nothing else can.

COOKING NOTES

Beans: canned vs. cooked from scratch

Beans of all sorts are one of the cornerstones of vegan and vegetarian soup making. They're not only a superb low-fat, high-fiber protein source, but also add great flavor and texture to soups. In instances where beans are the primary ingredient of a soup, such as in Black Bean Soup (page 38) or Spicy Chili Bean Stew (page 67), dried beans are called for, so that they become the base of the soup. In most cases where a smaller amount of cooked beans is needed, I specify canned beans. Busy cooks are loathe to take the time and trouble to cook a small amount of beans from scratch, unless, of course, the extra is saved for later use or for freezing. By all means, if you prefer to cook beans from scratch no matter what, I will not discourage you.

That said, I'd rather people use canned beans than forgo them altogether. There are several excellent organic brands to be found in natural food stores and well-stocked supermarkets. The advantage of these, aside from the obvious one (that they are organic), is that they are less salty than commercial brands. When using canned beans, I recommend draining and rinsing them of their salty liquid, which helps to mitigate the sodium factor. And of course, you can be more judicious when salting a soup that is made with canned beans.

Cooking equipment

The soups in this book are simple enough to require only the most basic of kitchen equipment. Aside from a large soup pot or Dutch oven, of course, the items needed are standard to most any kitchen: wooden spoons for stirring, a colander for washing leeks and leafy vegetables, a grater, measuring utensils, and good knives. For the devoted soup cook, I heartily recommend an immersion blender (see next page) or food processor for pureed soups; the food processor is also useful for making occasional grating easier and quicker.

Freezing soups

Some soups freeze well, but others lose much of their flavor and texture. Thick winter bean and grain soups do pretty well, as do simple broths and stocks. Freezing often changes the texture of a smooth puree, making it more watery. Avoid freezing soups that contain potatoes or lentils, both of which turn quite mushy. I don't recommend freezing soups containing raw ingredients, as in certain chilled soups. The soups in this book generally don't yield such enormous quantities to warrant long-term storage of leftovers. I prefer finishing most soups while they are fresh rather than after they have been frozen and thawed.

Immersion blender

This is a compact, inexpensive gadget featuring a small puree blade on the end of a wand. I love it and find it indispensable, not only for blending soups, but for making the fruit smoothies that we love in our household. Insert the blender into the pot of soup, press the button, and blend! It's also easy to clean and easy to store.

Oil and margarine

As you'll soon see, my oil of choice in most soups is olive oil. Unless extra-virgin is specified (in those instances when its more assertive flavor is desired), you can use any kind of lighter olive oil, such as pure. On occasion, I will call for nonhydrogenated margarine. My favorite brand is Earth Balance. If you shop mostly in the supermarket, its equivalent is Smart Balance, which is made by the same company.

Organic ingredients

I like to use organic produce exclusively. I like to support organic growers, and I do not want my family to ingest pesticides. I'm well aware that the standards for organic produce have been watered down, and that "drift" is an issue; however, by using organic produce as much as possible, it's a matter of doing the best that one can. I encourage you to do so, too. In the warmer months, our family belongs to an organic community farm that is just a mile from our home. Using local produce as much as possible is also kind to the earth, and having access to produce that was picked the same day it is used is the ultimate culinary pleasure. If you can't use organic produce all the time, use it as often as you can. I also recommend using organic grains as well as canned and frozen products. Canned tomatoes and beans, and frozen corn and peas are ingredients often used in soups, for instance, and organic versions of these and other products are excellent.

Seasonings for soups

The success of a meatless soup depends primarily on the flavor and freshness of its main ingredients, and next, on using a variety of seasonings, both dried and fresh. Dried seasonings are added early in the cooking process, of course, and fresh herbs at the end.

Quantities of seasonings given in soup recipes—in this book or others—should be tailored to individual tastes. As a perennial soup enthusiast, I have always loved to experiment with a pinch of this spice, a quarter teaspoon of this herb, and a half teaspoon of that. That's part of the fun and artistry of making soup.

After motherhood intervened, I enjoyed the practicality of making a big pot of soup that would last several days, but I began leaning toward recipes that could be made simply and quickly. The best time-saver I discovered was eliminating the need for measuring minute quantities of many herbs and spices and, instead, using purchased seasoning mixes whenever possible. Now that my sons are older and I can once again spend more time in the kitchen, I still enjoy the shortcuts afforded by spice blends, prepared broths, and broth starters like bouillon cubes and powders. There are many excellent natural brands—even organic options. They're readily available, they're tasty, and they're convenient. Why not use them?

There are many blends and brands around that are wonderfully suited to use in vegetarian and vegan soups, where small quantities of many seasonings add up to the zesty flavor needed to make any soup taste great. Feel free to experiment with the many varieties available. Here are the seasoning mixes I use most often in making soups:

Curry powder: Purchase this blend from a spice shop, natural food store, or Indian grocery, if possible. Use your sense of smell—curry powder should be fragrant and pungent. Different blends possess varying amounts of heat; how much is entirely up to your preference for hot vs. mild spiciness.

Italian herb seasoning: A blend of several herbs such as oregano, thyme, marjoram, and rosemary, this is commonly available at specialty outlets as well as supermarkets.

Salt-free seasoning: The savory blend of many different herbs and spices eliminates the need for excessive salting. This is an all-purpose way to add a complex flavor to soups. There are several good brands available in supermarkets and natural food stores. My favorites from the supermarket are salt-free Mrs. Dash Table Blend and McCormick Seasonings, which offers a few different all-purpose blends. From the natural food store, the aptly named Spike is a great product, as is Frontier All-Purpose Seasoning. There are other good brands; experiment with them and make good use of whichever you prefer.

Here are my favorite tips for seasoning soups and stews:

· Add salt toward the end of the cooking to give the other flavors a chance to develop and to avoid oversalting. Salt a little at a time, stir in thoroughly, and taste frequently.

· Those who need to limit their intake of salt might try adding lemon juice or more herbs and spices than called for.

· Where appropriate, a small amount of dry wine adds nice depth of flavor. I use wine in some of the soups, but you might like to experiment with it in other recipes.

· Add extra zest and heat to soups with minced fresh ginger. To my mind, even better than grating ginger from the root is to open a jar of minced ginger. As you know, fresh ginger can sometimes be dry and stringy. Ginger People is my favorite brand. It's finely and evenly minced, moist, and fresh tasting—perfect for soup and so very convenient.

· Most important, use the amount of seasoning given here as a guide. Use more or less to suit your own taste and the palates of those to whom you will be serving soups and stews.

Textures and consistencies

Soup making, though essentially very simple, is an inexact science. For instance, what one cook considers a large potato might seem medium-sized to another, and so the amount of water or liquid called for in a recipe might not always yield precise results. The soup recipes here often remind the cook to adjust the consistency or thickness, and this, like salting, should be done according to preference. Some soups are meant to be very thick, and others to be thin and brothy, but most seem to fall somewhere in between, and thus should be tailored to your liking.

NOTES ON INGREDIENTS

Dairy alternatives

Rice milk: In the previous editions of this book, I called for low-fat milk or soymilk as options for milky soups. But now that this book has "gone vegan," I totally prefer rice milk. Rice milk has a more neutral flavor, closer to the flavor and consistency of low-fat dairy milk. I think it just works better in soups than does soymilk, which has a somewhat sweet, "beany" undertone that is often too assertive, especially in delicately seasoned soups. Rice Dream Original Enriched is what I use. If, however, you have a preference for soymilk, that's your decision to make. Use plain soymilk wherever rice milk is specified.

Silk creamer: I call for this soy-based cream substitute in small amounts where a denser, creamy flavor is desired. Use the plain-flavored original, of course.

Nondairy cheeses and sour cream: For the few soups that previously called for cheese or soy cheese, I specify nondairy cheese in this edition. That's so readers can opt to use rice- or almond-based cheeses, as well as the more common soy cheese. Savvy vegans are well aware that many of these alternative cheeses contain a minute amount of casein, a milk protein that helps the cheese melt. Some vegans are comfortable with that, while others are not. My favorite brand is Vegan Gourmet, a meltable soy-based cheese made without casein. By the time this book sees print, it's possible that there will be other casein-free brands on the market.

Vegan sour cream: Most of the brands of nondairy sour cream are good for a start, but they are usually too clumpy coming out of their container. They need a little help to achieve a pleasant, sour cream–like texture. Please don't use the well-known national nondairy brand that starts with a "T." It occupies plenty of shelf space in many natural food stores, but is almost pure junk food. Here's a simple recipe giving you the option of starting with a ready-made nondairy sour cream, or using silken tofu to create a delicious vegan sour cream for that perfect dollop atop a bowl of soup.

Vegan Sour Cream

Makes a little more than 1 cup, about 8 servings

1 cup crumbled firm or extra-firm silken tofu,
or one 8-ounce container natural
nondairy sour cream

2 to 3 tablespoons rice milk or Silk creamer,
as needed

2 teaspoons lemon juice, or more to taste

¼ teaspoon salt, or to taste

Per serving:
Calories: 21   Total fat: 1 g   Protein: 2 g   Fiber: 0 g
Carbohydrate: 1 g   Cholesterol: 0 mg   Sodium: 88 mg

Combine all the ingredients in a food processor or the companion container to an immersion blender. Process until very smoothly pureed, then transfer to a container with an airtight lid. This keeps well for 3 to 4 days, refrigerated.

Of all the items on the menu, soup is that which exacts the most delicate perfection and the strictest attention.

—Auguste Escoffier (1846–1935)

Explanation of Nutritional Analyses

- All breakdowns are based on one serving. When a recipe gives a range in the number of servings, for example, 6 to 8 servings, the analysis is based on the average number of servings—in this example, 7 servings.

- When more than one ingredient is listed as an option, the first ingredient is used in the analysis. Usually, the optional ingredient will not change the analysis significantly.

- Ingredients listed as optional (for example, "chopped cashews for garnish, optional") are not included in the analysis.

- When a recipe gives a range for an ingredient to use, e.g., ¼ to ½ cup rice milk, the analysis is based on the lesser amount.

- When salt is listed "to taste," its sodium content is not included in the analysis.

- Canned tomato products are listed in 16- or 28-ounce quantities, though sometimes this may vary depending on brand. Imported tomato products often come in 14-ounce cans. The difference between using one or another in terms of the outcome of the analysis would be negligible, though please note that salt-free canned tomato products are specified. If you use a brand with sodium, that would definitely impact that portion of the analysis.

- In the recipes using canned beans, 16-ounce cans are called for, as that is what I figured would be most commonly used. I instruct the cook to drain and rinse the beans, which reduces the sodium content by about one-third. Please note that organic canned beans sometimes come in 15-ounce cans, and are almost always lower in sodium than commercial brands. If the latter is what you prefer to use, I would heartily recommend you continue to do so.

- The analyses provided in this book are sometimes based on using specific brands. When products are fairly generic, like salt-free diced tomatoes, it hardly matters what brand is used, in terms of the analyses. However, in a number of cases I had to make a decision to use a specific brand of a product for the analyses, since nutritional data varies somewhat from one to another. The outcome of any analysis won't be wildly different if you use a different brand of, let's say, soy cheese than I use, but I just want readers to know that there will be a slight difference in these cases.

STOCKS AND BROTHS

Contrary to culinary myth, the absence of a strong-flavored meat stock does not present a huge challenge to the creation of great soups and stews. Many ethnic cuisines produce classic soups that in their original form are completely vegetarian or vegan. True, almost any soup can benefit from a good stock to boost flavor, but I place fresh and flavorful ingredients and creative seasoning above stock in contributing to the success of a soup.

I would venture to say that most of the soup recipes in this book will work as well using water (with the help of a bouillon cube or two sometimes) as they will with a homemade or store-bought stock; still, it's useful to have stocks on hand when they're needed and to have a few basic recipes to refer to when you do have the inclination or a little extra time.

In the soup recipes in this book, I often list an amount of water needed plus a vegetable bouillon cube or two, as that is the simplest method. With all the fresh ingredients and flavorings in the soups, this is generally sufficient for achieving a good, rich flavor. Once in a while, especially for brothy Asian soups, I suggest a 32-ounce carton of low-sodium vegetable broth as my first choice. There are many good natural and even organic brands of this kind of soup starter. Here are a few more options for creating a good soup base:

Basic vegetable stock: Okay, if you are a purist, you can make your stock from scratch. You need to allow an extra hour before making the actual soup to prepare and cook this stock. Truth be told, I no longer do this, and I don't expect you to, either. But there will be some people who prefer making their own stock, and for those individuals, I provide a good basic recipe on page 11.

Water with bouillon cubes or soup base: The easiest and most economical option. Look for a no-salt-added brand. My favorite is Rapunzel Vegan Vegetable Bouillon. It's packed with flavor, organic, and has no added sodium. Each cube is actually equivalent to two standard-sized cubes.

Vegetable broth powder: A tablespoon of this type of stock enhancer goes a long way in a pot of soup. However, I don't recommend it in the ingredients listings, as it's more difficult to find a low-sodium variety of this product than either bouillon cubes or prepared broths. However, if you come across a low-salt brand with all-natural ingredients, by all means give it a try.

Prepared vegetable broth: As mentioned earlier, I sometimes call for this product for brothy Asian soups. I like to use a 32-ounce aseptic carton (Pacific Organic and Health Valley are two brands to look for, among others) rather than canned broth. But it's your choice; canned vegetable broth can also be a good option, if it is all natural and low in sodium or salt-free.

Following are a handful of stocks and broths, the first two of which are suitable as soup bases. The remaining ones, in the Asian tradition, make good broths to be eaten on their own or lightly embellished.

Basic Vegetable Stock

Makes about 6 cups

This is a basic stock that may be used in place of water in most any vegetable soup to give added depth of flavor. It's also a good way to use up vegetables that are limp or less than perfectly fresh.

7 cups water
1 large onion, chopped
2 to 3 cloves garlic, minced
1 large carrot, sliced
2 large celery stalks, sliced
1 medium potato, scrubbed and diced
1 cup coarsely shredded green cabbage
2 teaspoons salt-free seasoning (see page 4 for brands)

Per cup:
Calories: 48   Total fat: 1 g   Protein: 1 g   Fiber: 2 g
Carbohydrate: 11 g   Cholesterol: 0 mg   Sodium: 34 mg

Place all the ingredients in a large soup pot. Bring to a simmer, then cover and simmer gently over low heat for 40 to 45 minutes, or until the vegetables are quite tender. Strain the stock through a fine mesh strainer. Discard the solids or puree them and add to soup for a thicker consistency.

Soup breathes reassurance, it offers consolation; after a weary day it promotes sociability... There is nothing like a bowl of hot soup, its wisp of aromatic steam teasing the nostrils into quivering anticipation.

—Louis P. DeGouy
  The Soup Book, 1949

Onion and Garlic Broth

Makes about 6 cups

This broth may be used as an extra-flavorful soup stock or as an alternative, with a little extra kick, to Basic Vegetable Stock. It's also a soothing remedy for the common cold!

1 tablespoon olive oil
1 large onion, chopped, or 2 medium leeks, white parts only, chopped and well rinsed
4 to 6 cloves garlic, minced
¼ cup dry red wine
6 cups water

Per cup:
Calories: 42   Total fat: 2 g   Protein: 1 g   Fiber: 1 g
Carbohydrate: 4 g   Cholesterol: 0 mg   Sodium: 9 mg

Onion: Humble kindred of the lily clan, rooted from oblivion by Alexander the Great and bestrewn by him, along with learning, to the civilised world, thus lending a touch of wisdom and sophistication to the whole.

—Della Lutes
  The Country Kitchen, 1938

Heat the oil in a 2-quart saucepan or small soup pot. Add the onion or leeks and sauté over medium heat until golden.

Add the garlic and continue to sauté until the onion or leeks brown lightly. Add the wine and water. Bring to a simmer, then cover and simmer gently over low heat for 30 to 40 minutes. You may leave the onions and garlic in if you wish, or strain the stock through a fine strainer. Discard the solids or puree them and add to soup for a thicker consistency.

Simple Miso Broth

Makes about 6 cups

Miso is a nutritious, high-protein product fermented from soybeans and salt (or a combination of soybeans, grains, and salt). Available at all natural food stores and Asian groceries (as is the sea vegetable kombu), pungent-tasting miso is most commonly used to make simple broths. Here is a basic recipe, which really should be considered a soup in itself rather than as a stock for making other soups. Note that once the miso is stirred into water, it should not be boiled. Otherwise, its beneficial enzymes will be destroyed.

1 recipe Basic Vegetable Stock (page 11), or one 32-ounce carton low-sodium vegetable broth plus 2 cups water
2 strips kombu (sea vegetable), each about 3 by 5 inches
2 to 4 tablespoons miso, any variety, to taste

Per cup:
Calories: 42   Total fat: 2 g   Protein: 1 g   Fiber: 1 g
Carbohydrate: 4 g   Cholesterol: 0 mg   Sodium: 9 mg

Combine the stock and kombu in a 2-quart saucepan or small soup pot. Bring to a simmer.

Dissolve the desired amount of miso in just enough warm water to make it pourable. Stir into the broth and remove from the heat. Let stand for 30 minutes or serve at once, removing and discarding the kombu just before serving.

VARIATIONS:

Embellish miso broth with any of the following:
• Diced tofu
• Cooked Asian noodles
• Finely chopped scallions
• Grated fresh daikon radish or white turnip
• Crisp cucumber, seeded and grated

Basic Dashi

Makes about 6 cups

Like miso broth, dashi is another traditional Japanese stock that may be embellished in a number of ways, or eaten as is. It also makes a good base for certain Asian vegetable soups. Look for the sea vegetable kombu and dried shiitake mushrooms in Asian groceries or in natural food stores.

One 32-ounce carton low-sodium
    vegetable broth plus 2 cups water,
    or 6 cups water with 2 vegetable
    bouillon cubes
2 strips kombu (sea vegetable), each about
    3 by 7 inches
6 to 8 dried shiitake mushrooms

Per cup:
Calories: 23   Total fat: 0 g   Protein: 1 g   Fiber: 1 g
Carbohydrate: 5 g   Cholesterol: 0 mg   Sodium: 248 mg

Combine the broth and kombu in a 2-quart saucepan or small soup pot. Bring to a simmer.

Add the mushrooms to the broth, remove from the heat, and let stand for 30 minutes.

Remove the kombu from the broth and discard. Remove the mushrooms with a slotted spoon. Trim them of their tough stems and save the caps for another use, or slice them and return to the broth.

VARIATIONS:

Dashi with noodles: Simply cook a quantity of Asian noodles (like soba) in the broth. Once they are *al dente*, remove the soup from the heat, season to taste with natural soy sauce, and serve immediately. Garnish each serving with some finely chopped scallion.

Dashi with miso and vegetables: Use the broth to simmer any quantity of thinly sliced vegetables, such as carrot, cabbage, daikon radish, turnip, etc. Once the vegetables are just done, add 2 to 4 tablespoons miso, to taste, dissolved in just enough warm water to make it pourable. Stir in the sliced shiitake mushrooms from the preparation of the broth. Remove from the heat and serve at once.

Asian Mushroom Broth

Makes about 6 cups

This strong broth is a great flavor booster for Asian-style vegetable soups, and is also pleasing eaten on its own. Vary it by using any of the embellishments suggested under Simple Miso Broth (page 13).

2 teaspoons olive oil

1 small onion, minced

1 clove garlic, minced

One 32-ounce carton low-sodium vegetable broth plus 2 cups water, or 6 cups water with 2 vegetable bouillon cubes

8 to 10 dried shiitake mushrooms

1 to 2 tablespoons reduced-sodium soy sauce, to taste

Per cup:
Calories: 45   Total fat: 2 g   Protein: 1 g   Fiber: 1 g
Carbohydrate: 7 g   Cholesterol: 0 mg   Sodium: 330 mg

Heat the oil in a 2-quart saucepan or small soup pot. Add the onion and garlic and sauté over medium heat until golden.

Add the broth, mushrooms, and soy sauce. Bring to a simmer, then cover and simmer gently for 15 minutes.

Remove from the heat and let stand another 15 minutes. Strain through a sieve, reserving the mushrooms. Trim them of their tough stems. Save the caps for another use, or slice them and return to the broth.

FALL

Autumn is an inviting time to make soup. In early to midseason, the rich colors and lively flavors of the harvest can be shown off to great advantage in a warming pot of soup. Later in the season, a tasty bowl of soup is a heartwarming way to temper the effects of chilly weather.

Baked Onion Soup

A vegan take on the French classic, with bread and melted cheese

6 servings

Ceramic crocks with handles are the ideal bowls for this soup, but any type of ovenproof bowl will do. You'll cry a river while cutting the onions, but you and your family or guests will weep tears of joy while eating this heavenly soup.

2 tablespoons olive oil

8 medium onions, quartered and
    thinly sliced

2 cloves garlic, minced

2 cups water

One 32-ounce carton low-sodium vegetable
    broth, or other stock option (page 9)

¼ cup dry red wine

1 teaspoon dry mustard

Salt and freshly ground pepper to taste

Long narrow French or Italian bread,
    as needed

1½ cups grated mozzarella-style
    nondairy cheese

Per serving:
Calories: 307   Total fat: 15 g   Protein: 7 g   Fiber: 6 g
Carbohydrate: 37 g   Cholesterol: 0 mg   Sodium: 613 mg

Heat the oil in a soup pot. Add the onions and sauté over medium-low heat until golden. Add the garlic and continue to sauté slowly until the onions are lightly and evenly browned, stirring frequently, about 20 to 25 minutes.

Preheat the oven to 375 degrees.

Pour the water over the onions and give them a good stir. Then add the broth, wine, and mustard. Bring to a rapid simmer, then lower the heat. Cover and simmer gently for 15 minutes. Season with salt and pepper.

Meanwhile, cut the bread into 1-inch-thick slices, allowing 1 or 2 slices per serving depending on the size of your soup bowls. Bake for 15 minutes, or until dry and crisp, turning the slices over once about halfway through the baking time.

To assemble the soup, place one layer of bread (1 or 2 slices) in each ovenproof bowl and ladle a serving of soup over it. Sprinkle about ¼ cup of the grated cheese over each. Place the bowls on 1 or 2 sturdy baking sheets to make them easier to handle. Bake for approximately 10 minutes, or until the cheese is melted. Serve at once.

Happy is said to be the family which can eat onions together. They are, for the time being, separate from the world, and have a harmony of aspiration.

—Charles Dudley Warner
    My Summer in a Garden, 1871

Cream of White Vegetables

Pureed potatoes, white onions, and turnips with a colorful vegetable garnish

8 servings

A super-smooth, pale puree with a colorful garnish, this soup exudes both comfort and elegance. If you can, use the big, pure white onions that are abundant in the fall.

2 tablespoons olive oil

1½ pounds white onions (if unavailable, substitute yellow onions), chopped

1½ pounds white turnips, peeled and diced

3 large potatoes, peeled and diced

2 to 3 cloves garlic, minced

¼ to ½ cup rice milk, as needed

¼ cup Silk creamer

Salt and freshly ground pepper to taste

Garnish:

1 teaspoon olive oil

1 large red bell pepper, finely diced

½ cup frozen green peas, thawed

3 scallions, green parts only, sliced

¼ to ½ cup chopped fresh parsley

Per serving:
Calories: 170   Total fat: 5 g   Protein: 4 g   Fiber: 5 g
Carbohydrate: 29 g   Cholesterol: 0 mg   Sodium: 84 mg

Heat the oil in a soup pot. Add the onions and sauté over medium heat, covered, stirring occasionally, about 15 minutes, or until golden.

Set aside 1 cup of the turnip dice. Add the remaining turnips to the soup pot, followed by the potatoes and garlic. Add enough water to cover all but about ½ inch of the vegetables. Bring to a rapid simmer, then lower the heat. Cover and simmer gently until the vegetables are tender, about 30 to 40 minutes.

Transfer the vegetables to a food processor or blender with a slotted spoon and puree in batches until very smooth, then transfer back to the soup pot. Or insert an immersion blender into the pot and process until very smooth.

Stir in enough rice milk to give the soup a thick but fluid consistency. Stir in the creamer, then season with salt and pepper. Reheat very gently while preparing the garnish.

For the garnish, heat the oil in a medium-sized skillet. Add the bell pepper, reserved turnip dice, and about 2 tablespoons water. Cover and "sweat" over medium heat until tender-crisp, about 7 minutes. Add the peas, scallions, and parsley, and cook, covered, about 5 minutes longer, adding a bit more water if needed to keep the skillet moist.

Ladle the soup into bowls and divide the garnish among them, placing some in the center of each bowl of soup.

New England Clam-less Chowder

A mélange of potatoes and corn, with stand-ins for dairy and seafood

6 to 8 servings

Baked tofu is an excellent stand-in for clams in this classic American soup. I like to use mild-flavored Soy Boy Tofu Lin for this recipe, but you may use whatever brand or flavor you prefer.

2 tablespoons olive oil

1 large onion, finely chopped

2 celery stalks, finely diced

2 tablespoons unbleached white flour

4 cups water with 2 vegetable bouillon cubes, or other stock option (page 9)

3 medium potatoes, scrubbed and diced

3 cups thawed frozen or cooked fresh corn kernels (from about 3 large ears)

1 teaspoon salt-free seasoning (see page 4 for brands)

1 teaspoon ground cumin

4 ounces (½ package) baked tofu, finely diced

2 cups rice milk, or as needed

Salt and freshly ground pepper to taste

Per serving:
Calories: 229   Total fat: 7 g   Protein: 9 g   Fiber: 4 g
Carbohydrate: 38 g   Cholesterol: 0 mg   Sodium: 152 mg

Heat the oil in a soup pot. Add the onion and celery and sauté over medium heat until both are golden, about 8 to 10 minutes.

Sprinkle the flour over the onion and celery, a little at a time, and stir in. Slowly stir in the water with the bouillon cubes, potatoes, corn, seasoning, and cumin. Bring to a rapid simmer, then lower the heat. Cover and simmer gently until the potatoes are tender, about 20 to 25 minutes.

With the back of a wooden spoon, mash a small amount of the potatoes to thicken the base. Stir in the tofu, then add rice milk as needed; the soup should be somewhat thick but not overly dense.

Return to a gentle simmer, then season with salt and pepper. If time allows, let the soup stand off the heat for an hour or two, then heat through before serving.

Yukon Gold Potato Soup

with roasted garlic and red peppers

6 to 8 servings

Though this soup is low in fat, the buttery flavor of Yukon Gold potatoes makes it taste rich and luscious. Roasted garlic and red peppers add a deep, smoky flavor.

1 large or 2 medium whole heads garlic
1 tablespoon olive oil
1 cup finely chopped onion
6 to 7 medium Yukon Gold potatoes,
    peeled and diced
1 cup peeled, diced tender apple (such as
    Cortland or Golden Delicious)
¼ cup dry white wine
3 to 4 scallions, thinly sliced
One 6-ounce jar roasted red bell peppers,
    drained and cut into ½-inch squares
1 to 1½ cups rice milk, as needed
½ cup Silk creamer
Salt and freshly ground pepper to taste

Per serving:
Calories: 173   Total fat: 5 g   Protein: 3 g   Fiber: 3 g
Carbohydrate: 30 g   Cholesterol: 0 mg   Sodium: 85 mg

Preheat the oven to 350 degrees, or a toaster oven to 375 degrees. Place the whole garlic heads on a baking sheet and bake for 40 minutes.

Heat the oil in a soup pot. Add the onion and sauté over medium heat until golden. Add the potatoes, apple, wine, and just enough water to cover. Bring to a rapid simmer, then lower the heat. Cover and simmer gently for 25 to 30 minutes, or until the potato is quite tender.

When the garlic is done, squeeze the soft pulp from the cloves right into the soup and discard the skins. Mash the potatoes in the pot with a potato masher until the base is thick and chunky.

Add the scallions, roasted peppers, and enough rice milk to give the soup a thick consistency. Stir in the creamer and simmer gently for 5 minutes longer. Season with salt and pepper.

If time allows, let the soup stand off the heat for an hour. Before serving, heat through very gently. Adjust the consistency with more rice milk as needed, then taste to adjust the seasonings.

Potato, Cheese, and Green Chili Soup

A contemporary classic from the American Southwest

6 to 8 servings

*Here's a great soup to make in the early fall,
while fresh corn and tomatoes are still available.*

1 tablespoon olive oil

1 large onion, chopped

2 to 3 cloves garlic, minced

1 large green bell pepper, finely chopped

5 medium potatoes, peeled and diced

6 cups water with 2 vegetable bouillon cubes,
 or other stock option (page 9)

1 cup chopped fresh, ripe tomatoes

1 cup cooked fresh or thawed frozen
 corn kernels

½ cup chopped fresh mild green chilies,
 such as poblano

2 teaspoons ground cumin

1½ cups cheddar-style nondairy cheese,
 grated (this is great with Vegan
 Gourmet nacho cheese)

1 cup rice milk, or as needed

Salt and freshly ground pepper to taste

Per serving:
Calories: 234   Total fat: 11 g   Protein: 5 g   Fiber: 6 g
Carbohydrate: 33 g   Cholesterol: 0 mg   Sodium: 239 mg

Heat the oil in a soup pot. Add the onion and sauté over medium heat until translucent. Add the garlic and green pepper and continue to sauté until the mixture begins to brown lightly.

Add the potatoes and water with bouillon cubes. Bring to a rapid simmer, then lower the heat. Cover and simmer gently until the potatoes are just tender, about 15 minutes. Coarsely mash about half of the potatoes in the pot with a potato masher.

Stir in the tomatoes, corn, chilies, and cumin, then cover and simmer gently for another 15 minutes, stirring occasionally.

Sprinkle in the cheese, a little at a time, stirring it until fairly well melted. Add enough rice milk to give the soup a thick yet fluid consistency.

Season with salt and pepper and continue to simmer over very low heat, stirring occasionally, for 5 minutes longer. If time allows, let the soup stand off the heat for an hour or so. Heat through before serving. Adjust the consistency with more rice milk if the soup becomes too thick, then taste to adjust the seasonings.

Creamy Golden Potato-Squash Soup

A heavenly puree of hardy fall vegetables

6 to 8 servings

Onions, garlic, winter squash, and silken tofu are all enveloped in the familiar flavor of potatoes, making this a wonderful vehicle for getting a lot of nourishing ingredients into younger (or fussier) soup eaters.

1 medium acorn or golden acorn squash, about 1 pound

1 tablespoon olive oil

1 large onion, chopped

2 to 3 cloves garlic, minced

4 medium-large potatoes (about 1½ pounds), peeled and diced

2 bay leaves

2 vegetable bouillon cubes

½ teaspoon good-quality curry powder

½ teaspoon dried dill

One 12.3-ounce package firm silken tofu, coarsely crumbled

2 cups rice milk, or as needed

¼ cup Silk creamer, optional

Salt and freshly ground pepper to taste

Minced fresh parsley for garnish, optional

Per serving:
Calories: 203   Total fat: 5 g   Protein: 7 g   Fiber: 3 g
Carbohydrate: 35 g   Cholesterol: 0 mg   Sodium: 88 mg

Place the squash in a microwave-safe container. Microwave for 6 to 8 minutes, until it can be easily pierced with a knife. Or if you are using the oven for baking other foods, you can bake the squash in the oven. Cut it in half, wrap in foil, and bake at 375 or 400 degrees for 30 to 45 minutes, or until tender. Let the squash cool until it can be easily handled. Split it in half, remove the seeds and fibers, and scoop the flesh away from the skin. Set aside until needed.

Heat the oil in a soup pot. Add the onion and sauté over medium heat until golden. Add the garlic, potatoes, bay leaves, bouillon cubes, curry powder, and dill. Add enough water to just cover and bring to a simmer, then cover and simmer gently until the potatoes are tender, about 25 minutes.

Discard the bay leaves and add the squash and tofu. Transfer the solid ingredients to a food processor (in batches, if needed) and process until smoothly pureed, adding a little of the rice milk to each batch to soften the consistency. Return the puree to the pot and stir. Or insert an immersion blender into the pot and process until all the solid ingredients are smoothly pureed.

Stir in enough rice milk to give the soup a slightly thick consistency. Return to the heat and simmer over low heat until heated through, about 5 minutes. Stir in the optional creamer. Season with salt and pepper and serve. Or if time allows, let the soup stand off the heat for an hour or so, then heat through before serving. Garnish each serving with a little minced parsley, if desired.

Jerusalem Artichoke Puree
with potatoes and leeks

6 to 8 servings

Jerusalem artichokes (sometimes marketed as "sunchokes") are a hardy fall root vegetable. Their appealingly offbeat flavor and texture, something of a cross between potatoes and water chestnuts, will appeal to adventurous soup-makers. Barley or Rice Triangles (page 152) complement this soup nicely.

2 ½ tablespoons olive oil

1 large onion, chopped

2 cloves garlic, minced

1½ pounds Jerusalem artichokes, scrubbed, dark knobs trimmed away, and diced

2 medium potatoes, peeled and diced

¼ cup dry white wine

1 teaspoon good-quality curry powder

One 32-ounce carton low-sodium vegetable broth, or other stock option (page 9)

1 cup rice milk, more or less as needed

2 large leeks, white and palest green parts only

Juice of ½ to 1 lemon, to taste

Salt and freshly ground pepper to taste

¼ cup minced fresh parsley, or more to taste

Per serving:
Calories: 200   Total fat: 5 g   Protein: 4 g   Fiber: 3 g
Carbohydrate: 35 g   Cholesterol: 0 mg   Sodium: 230 mg

Heat 1 tablespoon of the oil in a large soup pot. Add the onion and sauté over medium-low heat until translucent. Add the garlic and continue to sauté until both are golden.

Reserve and set aside about one-third of the diced Jerusalem artichokes. Place the rest in a soup pot along with the potatoes, wine, curry powder, and broth. Bring to a rapid simmer, then lower the heat. Cover and simmer gently until the vegetables are tender, about 20 minutes.

With a slotted spoon, transfer the solid ingredients to a food processor and puree, in batches if necessary, until smooth. Return the puree to the soup pot. Or simply insert an immersion blender into the pot and puree until smooth.

Add enough rice milk to give the soup a medium-thick consistency. Return to low heat and simmer very gently.

Meanwhile, cut the leeks in half, then into ¼-inch slices. Separate the rings of the leeks and rinse well to remove grit. Heat the remaining oil in a skillet. Add the leeks and about 2 tablespoons water. Sauté over medium-low heat until limp.

Add the reserved artichoke dice to the skillet. Raise the heat to medium and sauté with the leeks, stirring frequently, until both are just beginning to brown lightly. Remove from the heat, then stir the leeks and artichokes into the soup.

Season with lemon juice, salt, and pepper. If time allows, let the soup stand for an hour or so before serving, then heat through. Garnish each serving with a sprinkling of parsley.

Hot Beet and Potato Borscht

with citrus notes and fresh dill

6 to 8 servings

Though beet borscht is generally eaten cold, the addition of potatoes creates a more robust version for fall or winter. Onion-Rye Scones (page 155) complement this soup well. Unless you are fond of hand grating, using a food processor makes the job much easier.

1½ tablespoons olive oil

2 large onions, chopped

3 medium potatoes, peeled and grated

4 medium beets, peeled and grated

1 large carrot, peeled and grated

1 cup orange juice, freshly squeezed
     or store-bought organic

Juice of 1 lemon

2 tablespoons minced fresh dill

2 to 3 tablespoons natural granulated sugar,
     more or less to taste

Salt and freshly ground pepper to taste

Vegan Sour Cream (page 7), optional

Per serving:
Calories: 143   Total fat: 3 g   Protein: 3 g   Fiber: 3 g
Carbohydrate: 30 g   Cholesterol: 0 mg   Sodium: 40 mg

Heat the oil in a soup pot. Add the onion and sauté over medium heat until golden. Add all the remaining ingredients except the sugar, salt and pepper, and optional sour cream.

Add enough water to cover the vegetables. Bring to a rapid simmer, then lower the heat. Cover and simmer gently until the vegetables are tender, about 40 minutes.

Adjust the consistency with more water if the soup is too dense. Season with sugar, salt, and pepper, then simmer for 5 minutes longer.

If time allows, let the soup stand for an hour or two. Heat through before serving. Garnish each serving with a dollop of sour cream, if desired.

To be a maker of good soups one must not only have skill and patience, but must also use good materials ... Soup should be palatable and nutritious. If these qualities be lacking, there will be no excuse for serving it. Knowledge and care must be applied in combining the various ingredients in order to secure results at once pleasing and healthful.

—Maria Parloa
   Miss Parloa's Kitchen Companion, 1887

Mellow Sweet Potato Soup

Subtly spiced and not quite pureed

6 servings

This warming soup tempts the eye with an appealing golden color, and pleases the palate with the delectable flavor of sweet potatoes.

2 tablespoons olive oil

2 medium onions, chopped

2 medium carrots, peeled and diced

1 large celery stalk, diced

Handful of celery leaves

6 cups peeled, diced sweet potatoes (about
    3 to 4 medium-large)

2 bay leaves

¼ teaspoon dried thyme

¼ teaspoon ground nutmeg

1 cup rice milk, or as needed

¼ cup Silk creamer

Salt and freshly ground pepper to taste

Per serving:
Calories: 236   Total fat: 7 g   Protein: 3 g   Fiber: 5 g
Carbohydrate: 43 g   Cholesterol: o mg   Sodium: 56 mg

Heat the oil in a soup pot. Add the onions, carrots, and celery and sauté over low heat until all are golden.

Add the celery leaves and sweet potato dice. Add just enough water to cover all but about an inch of the vegetables. Bring to a rapid simmer, stir in the bay leaves and seasonings, then lower the heat. Cover and simmer until the sweet potatoes and vegetables are tender, about 20 to 25 minutes.

Discard the bay leaves. Remove about half of the solid ingredients with a slotted spoon and transfer to a food processor along with about ½ cup of the cooking liquid. Process until smoothly pureed, then stir back into the soup pot. Or insert an immersion blender into the pot and puree about half the ingredients.

Add enough rice milk to give the soup a slightly thick consistency, then stir in the creamer. Season with salt and pepper. Simmer over very low heat for another 10 to 15 minutes.

Serve at once, or if time allows, let stand off the heat for an hour or two. Heat through before serving.

Curried Red Lentil Soup

with sweet potatoes and greens

6 servings

Both nourishing and sublimely satisfying, this thick soup incorporates fall's first sweet potatoes with seasonal greens. Red lentils, which cook to a warm golden color, are available in natural food stores and ethnic groceries. Serve with Chapatis (page 158) or a store-bought flatbread.

2 tablespoons olive oil

1 cup chopped red onion

2 cloves garlic, minced

6 cups water

1½ cups dried red lentils, rinsed and sorted

2 large or 3 medium sweet potatoes, peeled and diced

1 teaspoon grated fresh ginger

2 teaspoons good-quality curry powder, more or less to taste

½ teaspoon ground coriander

¼ teaspoon cinnamon

¼ teaspoon ground nutmeg

6 to 8 ounces Swiss chard or spinach

Juice of 1 lemon or lime

Salt to taste

Per serving:
Calories: 290   Total fat: 5 g   Protein: 13 g   Fiber: 10 g
Carbohydrate: 50 g   Cholesterol: 0 mg   Sodium: 94 mg

Heat the oil in a soup pot. Add the onion and garlic and sauté over medium heat until golden, about 10 minutes. Add the water, followed by the lentils, sweet potatoes, and seasonings. Bring to a rapid simmer, then lower the heat. Cover and simmer gently until the lentils are mushy and the potatoes are done, about 20 to 25 minutes.

Meanwhile, wash the greens, remove stems and midribs, then slice into narrow shreds. Stir into the soup along with the lemon juice. If the soup is too thick, adjust the consistency with a small amount of water.

Continue to simmer gently until the greens are just done, about 5 minutes for spinach and 10 to 15 minutes for chard. Season with salt. Serve at once, or if time allows, let the soup stand off the heat for an hour or two. Heat through before serving.

Kale, Yellow Squash, and Sweet Potato Stew

A sturdy mélange of colorful seasonal veggies

6 to 8 servings

As everyone knows, greens are good for you, but with its high calcium content, kale is a standout. Unlike many greens, kale does not wilt on contact with heat, but needs a good bit of simmering to get done. Its deep green color and elaborately ruffled leaves, contrasted with the yellow of the squash and the orange of the sweet potato, make this an attractive and nourishing dish for the early autumn harvest.

1½ cups water

⅔ cup short- or medium-grain raw brown rice, rinsed

1 tablespoon olive oil

1 medium-large red onion, chopped

2 cloves garlic, minced

6 to 8 ounces fresh kale

2 to 3 medium sweet potatoes, peeled and diced

4 cups water with 2 vegetable bouillon cubes, or one 32-ounce carton low-sodium vegetable broth

½ teaspoon grated fresh ginger

1 teaspoon dry mustard

2 small yellow summer squash, diced

2 medium ripe tomatoes, diced

2 tablespoons balsamic vinegar, or to taste

Salt and freshly ground pepper to taste

Per serving:
Calories: 165   Total fat: 3 g   Protein: 4 g   Fiber: 4 g
Carbohydrate: 31 g   Cholesterol: 0 mg   Sodium: 70 mg

Bring 1½ cups water to a boil in a small saucepan. Stir in the rice, then cover and simmer gently until done, about 35 minutes.

Meanwhile, heat the oil in a soup pot. Add the onion and sauté over medium-low heat until translucent. Add the garlic and continue to sauté until both are golden.

Trim away and discard the thick midribs from the kale leaves. Chop the kale into bite-sized pieces and rinse well in a colander. Add to the soup pot along with the sweet potatoes and water with bouillon cubes. Add the ginger and mustard and stir well. Bring to a rapid simmer, then lower the heat. Cover and simmer gently for about 10 minutes.

Stir in the squash and tomatoes and simmer until the kale and sweet potato dice are tender, about 15 to 20 minutes. Mash enough of the sweet potato dice with the back of a wooden spoon to thicken the base.

Season with balsamic vinegar, salt, and pepper. If time allows, let the stew stand off the heat for an hour or two. Heat through before serving.

Miso–Butternut Squash Soup
with soba noodles and spinach

6 servings

Once you've got the squash baked, this Japanese-style soup comes together quickly, and is as pleasing to the eye as it is to the palate. Use chopsticks for "slurping" the noodles.

1 small butternut squash, about 1 pound

3 cups water

4 ounces soba (buckwheat noodles),
    broken in half

½ to 1 teaspoon grated fresh ginger, to taste

One 15-ounce can low-sodium
    vegetable broth

5 to 6 ounces fresh baby spinach, stemmed
    and rinsed

1 cup frozen green peas, thawed

2 to 3 tablespoons miso, any variety

Freshly ground pepper to taste

Per serving:
Calories: 153   Total fat: 1 g   Protein: 7 g   Fiber: 6 g
Carbohydrate: 33 g   Cholesterol: 0 mg   Sodium: 519 mg

Place the squash in a microwave-safe container. Microwave for 8 minutes, or until it can be easily pierced with a knife but is still firm. Or if you are using the oven for baking other foods, you can bake the squash in the oven. Cut it in half, wrap in foil, and bake at 375 or 400 degrees for 30 to 45 minutes, or until tender. Either way, this step can be done ahead of time. Let the squash cool until it can be easily handled. Split it in half, remove the seeds and fibers, and scoop the flesh away from the skin. Cut into large dice and set aside until needed.

Bring the water to a simmer in a soup pot. Add the soba and ginger and cook until the noodles are *al dente*.

Add the broth, spinach, peas, and diced squash. Cook just until the spinach is wilted but still bright green and everything is well heated through.

Dissolve the miso in ⅓ cup warm water and stir into the soup, then taste. If you'd like to add more miso, dissolve a small amount in a little warm water before adding. Season with pepper and serve at once.

Orange–Butternut Squash Soup
with sautéed turnips and red onions

6 servings

*This cheerfully colored soup brings you a hint
of sweetness and the pleasant crunch of turnips.
Once you've got the squash baked, the rest is
a snap.*

1 large butternut squash, about 2 pounds

2 tablespoons olive oil or fragrant nut oil
    (such as walnut)

1 large red onion, quartered and thinly sliced

3 cups water

1 cup freshly squeezed or good-quality
    orange juice

2 cups frozen green peas, thawed

3 to 4 scallions, white and green parts, thinly
    sliced

1 teaspoon good-quality curry powder

1 teaspoon grated fresh ginger

¼ teaspoon cinnamon

Pinch of ground nutmeg

2 medium turnips, peeled and cut into
    ½-inch dice

Salt and freshly ground pepper to taste

Per serving:
Calories: 213   Total fat: 5 g   Protein: 6 g   Fiber: 11 g
Carbohydrate: 40 g   Cholesterol: 0 mg   Sodium: 95 mg

Preheat the oven to 375 degrees. Halve the squash
lengthwise and place cut side up in a foil-lined shallow
baking dish. Cover with more foil. Bake for 45 to 50
minutes, or until soft. This step can be done as much as
a day ahead of time.

When the squash is cool enough to handle, scoop out
and discard the seeds and fibers. Scoop the flesh away
from the skin and transfer to a food processor.

Heat 1 tablespoon of the oil in a soup pot. Add the onion
and sauté over medium-low heat until golden, stirring
frequently. Remove half of the onion and set aside.
Transfer the remaining half to the food processor, and
process with the squash until the mixture is smoothly
pureed.

Transfer the puree to the soup pot. Add the water and
the orange juice and stir together. Bring to a gentle
simmer, then add the remaining ingredients except
the last two and the reserved onion. Cover and simmer
gently for 10 minutes.

Meanwhile, heat the remaining oil in a medium-sized
skillet. Add the turnips and sauté over medium-high
heat until touched with golden spots, stirring frequently.

Stir the turnips and reserved onion into the soup. Season
with salt and pepper. If needed, adjust the consistency
with more water or orange juice, then adjust the
seasonings. The soup should have a thick but flowing
consistency. Simmer very gently for 5 minutes longer.

Serve at once, or if time allows, let the soup stand off the
heat for an hour or two. Heat through before serving.

Spaghetti Squash Stew
with turnips and snow peas

8 servings

If it's possible for squash to be considered a "fun" food, spaghetti squash certainly fits that description. Its noodlelike strands contrast nicely with the crisp turnips and snow peas in this stew.

1 medium spaghetti squash

2 tablespoons olive oil

1 large onion, quartered and thinly sliced

2 cloves garlic, minced

One 28-ounce can salt-free diced tomatoes, undrained

¼ cup minced oil-cured sun-dried tomatoes

2 cups water

1 cup small mushrooms, thinly sliced

2 teaspoons salt-free seasoning (see page 4 for brands)

½ teaspoon dried oregano

¼ teaspoon dried thyme

Salt and freshly ground pepper to taste

1 pound turnips, peeled and cut into thick matchsticks

2 cups snow peas, trimmed and cut in half crosswise

Per serving:
Calories: 134   Total fat: 5 g   Protein: 3 g   Fiber: 5 g
Carbohydrate: 20 g   Cholesterol: 0 mg   Sodium: 90 mg

Preheat the oven to 375 degrees.

Cut the squash in half lengthwise, then scrape out the seeds. Place the two halves, cut side up, in a foil-lined shallow baking dish. Cover tightly with more foil and bake for 40 to 50 minutes, or until easily pierced with a fork.

When the squash is cool enough to handle, scrape the flesh away from the shell with a fork, using long downward motions to remove the spaghettilike strands.

Heat 1 tablespoon of the oil in a soup pot. Add the onion and sauté over medium heat until translucent. Add the garlic and continue to sauté until the onion is golden and just beginning to brown.

Add the spaghetti squash, canned and dried tomatoes, water, mushrooms, seasoning, oregano, and thyme. Bring to a rapid simmer, then lower the heat. Cover and simmer gently for 20 to 25 minutes. Season with salt and pepper.

Meanwhile, heat the remaining tablespoon of oil in a skillet. Add the turnips and sauté over medium-high heat, stirring frequently, until golden. Add the snow peas and continue to sauté, stirring, until the snow peas are bright green and tender-crisp. Top each serving with some of the turnips and snow peas, and serve at once.

Pumpkin-Apple Soup
with sweet spices and toasted nuts

6 to 8 servings

Make this soup a few hours ahead of time, if you can. The unusual combination of flavors benefits from having time to blend. You can use butternut squash instead of pumpkin, if you prefer.

1 sugar pumpkin, about 2 pounds

1½ tablespoons olive oil

1 large onion, finely chopped

2 medium celery stalks, finely diced

2 medium tart apples, peeled, cored, and diced

4 cups water with 1 vegetable bouillon cube, or other stock option (page 9)

1 teaspoon grated fresh ginger

1 teaspoon good-quality curry powder

½ teaspoon cinnamon

¼ teaspoon ground nutmeg

2 cups rice milk, or as needed

¼ cup Silk creamer, optional

Salt and freshly ground pepper to taste

½ cup chopped toasted almonds or cashews for garnish

Minced fresh parsley for garnish, optional

Per serving:

Calories: 172 Total fat: 8 g Protein: 4 g Fiber: 5 g
Carbohydrate: 25 g Cholesterol: 0 mg Sodium: 60 mg

Preheat the oven to 375 degrees. Halve the pumpkin lengthwise and place cut side up in a foil-lined shallow baking dish. Cover with more foil. Bake for 45 to 50 minutes, or until easily pierced with a knife. This step can be done as much as a day ahead of time. When cool enough to handle, scoop out and discard the seeds and fibers. Peel and cut the flesh into large dice.

Heat the oil in a soup pot. Add the onion and celery and sauté over medium heat until golden. Add the pumpkin, apples, water with bouillon cube, and seasonings. Bring to a rapid simmer, then lower the heat. Cover and simmer gently for 20 to 25 minutes, or until the pumpkin and apple are completely tender.

Transfer the solid ingredients to a food processor and puree completely, or leave it rather chunky. You can also puree just half of the solid ingredients for a more textured soup, if you prefer. Transfer back to the soup pot. Or insert an immersion blender into the soup pot and process to the desired consistency.

Stir in enough rice milk to give the soup a slightly thick consistency. Stir in the optional creamer, then season with salt and pepper and remove from the heat.

Serve at once, or allow the soup to stand off the heat for an hour or two. Taste to adjust the seasonings, then heat through before serving. Garnish each serving with a sprinkling of chopped nuts and parsley, if desired.

Moroccan-Style Vegetable Stew
with winter squash, chickpeas, and couscous

6 or more servings

This delicious stew looks and smells as enticing as it tastes. My sister-in-law, Toni Atlas, provided the inspiration for this recipe.

1½ tablespoons olive oil

2 large onions, chopped

2 medium potatoes, scrubbed and cut into
 ¾-inch chunks

2 heaping cups sugar pumpkin or
 butternut squash, peeled and cut into
 ¾-inch chunks (see Note)

2 large carrots, peeled and coarsely chopped

One 16-ounce can salt-free diced tomatoes,
 undrained

2 teaspoons ground cumin

½ teaspoon turmeric

One 16-ounce can chickpeas, drained
 and rinsed

Salt and freshly ground pepper to taste

2 cups water

1 cup raw couscous, preferably whole-grain

¼ to ½ cup minced fresh parsley, to taste

Per serving:
Calories: 300   Total fat: 5 g   Protein: 10 g   Fiber: 10 g
Carbohydrate: 55 g   Cholesterol: 0 mg   Sodium: 130 mg

Heat the oil in a soup pot. Add the onions and sauté over medium heat until golden.

Add the potatoes, pumpkin or squash, carrots, tomatoes, cumin, and turmeric. Add enough water to cover all but about ½ inch of the vegetables. Bring to a rapid simmer, then lower the heat. Cover and simmer gently for 35 to 40 minutes, or until the vegetables are tender.

Stir in the chickpeas, then season with salt and pepper. Simmer over very low heat for 10 to 15 minutes longer.

Meanwhile, bring the water to a boil in a small saucepan. Stir in the couscous, cover, and remove from the heat. Let stand for 10 minutes, then fluff with a fork.

To serve the stew, place a small amount of the couscous in each soup bowl, then ladle some stew over it and sprinkle with parsley. Serve at once.

NOTE:
I find that partially baking or briefly microwaving sugar pumpkin or squash makes it much easier to peel and dice. In this case, a very small pumpkin or squash would more than suffice, and microwaving for about 4 to 5 minutes would do the trick. Make sure the pumpkin or squash is cool enough before handling.

Moroccan Lentil and Chickpea Soup
Two flavorful legumes in a gently spiced broth

6 servings

This soup (called *harira* in Arabic) presents a compatible duo of lentils and chickpeas. It can be served all year round, but is especially appealing as a transitional early fall soup, using fresh tomatoes. Serve with fresh pita bread.

2 tablespoons olive oil
1 large onion, finely chopped
3 large celery stalks, diced
2 cloves garlic, minced
¾ cup dried lentils, rinsed and sorted
1 teaspoon turmeric
1 teaspoon ground cumin
1 teaspoon grated fresh ginger
½ teaspoon cinnamon
6 cups water
2 cups diced ripe tomatoes
One 16-ounce can chickpeas,
    drained and rinsed
Juice of ½ lemon (slice the remainder
    thinly for an optional garnish)
¼ cup chopped fresh parsley, or more to taste
Salt and freshly ground pepper to taste

Per serving:
Calories: 219   Total fat: 6 g   Protein: 10 g   Fiber: 9 g
Carbohydrate: 32 g   Cholesterol: 0 mg   Sodium: 155 mg

Heat the oil in a soup pot. Add the onion and sauté over medium heat until translucent, about 5 minutes. Add the celery and garlic and sauté until the onion is golden, about 5 to 7 minutes.

Add the lentils, spices, and water. Bring to a rapid simmer, then lower the heat. Cover and simmer gently until the lentils are just tender, about 30 to 35 minutes.

Stir in the tomatoes and chickpeas. Adjust the consistency with more water if needed, and adjust the spices to taste. Simmer for 10 to 15 minutes longer over very low heat.

Stir in the lemon juice and parsley, then season with salt and pepper. Serve hot or just warm, garnishing each serving with one or two thin lemon slices, if desired.

Chickpea and Tahini Soup

with mushrooms and lots of fresh herbs

6 to 8 servings

The classic Middle Eastern team of chickpeas and tahini (sesame paste) is combined in a tasty, offbeat soup. Serve with fresh whole wheat pita bread. Middle Eastern bulgur salad (tabbouleh) and a steamed green vegetable round this meal out nicely.

1 tablespoon olive oil

1 medium onion, chopped

3 to 4 cloves garlic, minced

4 cups water with 2 vegetable bouillon cubes, or other stock option (page 9)

2 cups sliced white, baby bella, or crimini mushrooms

1 cup finely shredded green cabbage

1 teaspoon ground cumin

2 teaspoons salt-free seasoning (see page 4 for brands)

Two 16-ounce cans chickpeas, drained and rinsed

¼ cup tahini

¼ to ½ cup finely chopped fresh parsley, to taste

3 to 4 scallions, green parts only, thinly sliced

2 to 3 tablespoons minced fresh dill, or more to taste

Juice of ½ to 1 lemon, to taste

Salt and freshly ground pepper to taste

Per serving:
Calories: 247   Total fat: 11 g   Protein: 10 g   Fiber: 11 g
Carbohydrate: 31 g   Cholesterol: 0 mg   Sodium: 280 mg

Heat the oil in a soup pot. Add the onion and garlic and sauté over medium-low heat until golden.

Add the water with bouillon cubes, mushrooms, cabbage, and seasonings. Bring to a rapid simmer, then lower the heat. Cover and simmer gently for 15 minutes.

Meanwhile, set aside 1 cup of the chickpeas and place the remainder in a food processor or blender with the tahini. Add a little water as needed to thin the consistency. Process until smoothly pureed. Stir the puree into the soup pot.

Stir in the reserved chickpeas, bring to a simmer, then cover and simmer very gently for 10 minutes.

Stir in the parsley, scallions, dill, and lemon juice. Add water as needed for a medium-thick consistency.

Season with salt and pepper, then simmer for 5 minutes longer. Serve at once, or let stand off the heat for an hour or two. Heat through before serving.

Chickpeas are under the dominion of Venus. They are less windy than beans, but nourish more ... they have a cleansing facility.

—Nicolas Culpeper (1616–1654)
  Culpeper's Complete Herbal

Southwestern Fresh Corn Stew
with green beans and chilies

6 servings

While fresh local corn is abundant in early fall, the most tempting way to eat it is right off the cob. But cooking with fresh corn can be equally appealing. Its sweetness and crunch can't be matched by frozen corn kernels. Serve this with Hearty Bean Bread (page 146) and a green salad for a filling meal.

1 tablespoon olive oil

1 large onion, chopped

2 to 3 cloves garlic, minced

4 medium ears fresh corn

2 medium ripe tomatoes, diced

One 16-ounce can salt-free pureed or
   crushed tomatoes

2 small yellow summer squash, cut into
   ¾-inch dice

1½ to 2 cups fresh slender green beans,
   trimmed and cut into 1-inch lengths
   (see Note)

1 to 2 fresh mild chilies (such as Anaheim or
   poblano), seeded and minced

3 cups water, or as needed

¼ to ½ cup finely chopped fresh cilantro,
   to taste

Salt and freshly ground pepper to taste

Vegan Sour Cream (page 7) for topping,
   optional

Per serving:
Calories: 138   Total fat: 3 g   Protein: 5 g   Fiber: 6 g
Carbohydrate: 27 g   Cholesterol: 0 mg   Sodium: 46 mg

Heat the oil in a soup pot. Add the onion and garlic and sauté over medium-low heat until golden.

Scrape the corn kernels from the cobs with a sharp knife. Add them to the soup pot, along with the fresh and canned tomatoes, squash, green beans, and chilies.

Add the water, more or less as needed for a moist but not too soupy consistency. Bring to a rapid simmer, then lower the heat. Cover and simmer gently for 20 minutes, or until the vegetables are tender.

Stir in the cilantro, then season with salt and pepper. Simmer very gently for 5 minutes more. Serve at once, topping each serving with sour cream, if desired.

NOTE:
If you can't find green beans that look fresh and tender, use frozen green beans. Thaw them completely before using.

VARIATION:
Add a cup or two of cooked pinto or pink beans to the stew and serve with a fresh, multigrain bread instead of the Hearty Bean Bread suggested in the headnote.

Never blow your soup if it is too hot, but wait until it cools. Never raise your plate to your lips, but eat it with your spoon.

—C.B. Hartley
   The Gentleman's Book of Etiquette, 1873

Autumn Harvest Stew

A tribute to the "three sisters"—corn, squash, and beans

8 servings

This colorful stew is an autumnal cousin to chili, using Native American ingredients. It's a good dish to try out on older kids and teens who have begun to appreciate more complex combinations of flavors and ingredients.

1 tablespoon olive oil

1 large onion, chopped

2 cloves garlic, minced

1 medium red or green bell pepper, diced

1 cup water

4 heaping cups prebaked, peeled, and diced orange squash (sugar pumpkin, butternut, carnival, etc.)

3 cups corn kernels (preferably fresh, scraped from 3 to 4 ears)

One 28-ounce can salt-free diced tomatoes, undrained

One 16-ounce can red or black beans, drained and rinsed

1 to 2 fresh hot chilies, seeded and minced, or one 4-ounce can chopped mild green chilies

2 teaspoons ground cumin

1 teaspoon dried oregano

Salt and freshly ground pepper to taste

Per serving:
Calories: 193   Total fat: 3 g   Protein: 8 g   Fiber: 10 g
Carbohydrate: 40 g   Cholesterol: 0 mg   Sodium: 110 mg

Heat the oil in a soup pot or steep-sided stir-fry pan. Add the onion and sauté over medium heat until translucent. Add the garlic and bell pepper and continue to sauté until the onion is golden.

Add all the remaining ingredients except the salt and pepper. Bring to a rapid simmer, then lower the heat. Cover and simmer gently for 15 to 20 minutes. Season gently with salt and pepper, then serve in shallow bowls.

We dined on Indian corn and Squash soup, and boiled bread.

—John Bartram
Observations in His Travels, 1751

Long-Simmering Black Bean Soup
The American classic—robust and brimming with complex flavors

6 to 8 servings

With any of the muffins, pages 149 to 151, and a simple salad, this soup is the basis of a filling and hearty meal. I especially like this with Cheese and Herb Corn Muffins (page 150).

1 pound dried black beans, rinsed and sorted

1 cup chopped onion

2 large carrots, peeled and chopped

2 large celery stalks, diced

2 or 3 cloves garlic, crushed or minced

¼ cup chopped fresh parsley

2 bay leaves

2 teaspoons salt-free seasoning
   (see page 4 for brands)

¼ teaspoon ground nutmeg

¼ cup dry red wine or sherry, optional

Salt and freshly ground pepper to taste

Garnishes:

1 tablespoon olive oil

1 large onion, quartered and thinly sliced

1 lemon, thinly sliced

Finely chopped fresh parsley

Per serving:

Calories: 277 Total fat: 3 g Protein: 15 g Fiber: 12 g
Carbohydrate: 50 g Cholesterol: 0 mg Sodium: 28 mg

Soak the beans overnight in plenty of water in a large covered soup pot. Or cover with water, bring to a boil, then let stand off the heat for an hour for a shortcut version of presoaking.

In either case, drain the beans after soaking, and rinse. Place in a soup pot with fresh water in a ratio of approximately 3 parts water to 1 part beans. Bring to a simmer, then cover and simmer steadily for 1 hour.

Add the onion, carrots, celery, garlic, parsley, bay leaves, seasoning, nutmeg, and optional wine. Simmer for another 1 to 1½ hours, or until the beans are soft.

Scoop out about 1½ cups of the beans with a slotted spoon, avoiding as much as possible scooping out the other vegetables. Set aside.

Discard the bay leaves and transfer the solid ingredients, in batches, to a food processor or blender. Use about ¼ cup cooking liquid per batch. Process until smoothly pureed, then return the puree to the soup pot along with the reserved beans. Or insert an immersion blender into the pot and process until smoothly pureed. Season with salt and pepper and return to low heat for 15 minutes.

Just before serving, heat the oil in a small skillet. Add the sliced onion and sauté over medium heat until golden brown.

Garnish each serving with some of the sautéed onion, 2 lemon slices, and some chopped parsley. This soup keeps very well for several days, and the flavor improves as it stands.

Beans possess over all vegetables the great advantage of being just as good, if not better, when kept waiting, an advantage in the case of people whose disposition or occupation makes it difficult for them to be punctual.

—André Simon
  The Concise Dictionary of Gastronomy, 1952

Almond–Brussels Sprouts Soup

with hints of wine and lemon

6 to 8 servings

Elegant and richly flavored, this soup features almond butter as its base. Fresh whole-grain bread and a salad of tomatoes and mixed greens make excellent companions.

1 tablespoon olive oil

1 large onion, chopped

1 large celery stalk, chopped

1 clove garlic, minced

1 large potato, peeled and diced

⅓ cup dry white wine

1 large tomato, diced

1½ pounds brussels sprouts, trimmed and
    coarsely chopped

4 cups water with 2 vegetable bouillon cubes,
    or other stock option (page 9)

2 teaspoons salt-free seasoning
    (see page 4 for brands)

½ cup almond butter

2 tablespoons lemon juice, more or less
    to taste

Salt and freshly ground pepper to taste

Chopped fresh parsley for garnish

Slivered or chopped almonds for garnish,
    optional

Per serving:
Calories: 224   Total fat: 14 g   Protein: 8 g   Fiber: 6 g
Carbohydrate: 21 g   Cholesterol: 0 mg   Sodium: 77 mg

Heat the oil in a soup pot. Add the onion and celery and sauté over medium heat until golden.

Add the garlic, potato, wine, tomato, about two thirds of the brussels sprouts (reserve and set aside the remainder), water with bouillon cubes, and seasoning. Bring to a rapid simmer, then lower the heat. Cover and simmer gently for 30 to 35 minutes, or until all the vegetables are tender. Remove from the heat.

Transfer the solid ingredients to a food processor and puree, in batches if necessary, until smooth. Transfer back to the soup pot, and whisk in the almond butter until smoothly integrated into the stock. Or add the almond butter, then insert an immersion blender into the pot and puree the soup until smooth. If needed, add enough water to give the soup a smooth, medium-thick consistency. Return to very low heat.

In a separate saucepan, steam the reserved brussels sprouts in about ½ inch of water until they are bright green and tender-crisp. Stir them into the soup. Season with lemon juice, salt, and pepper.

Serve at once. Garnish each serving with a sprinkling each of parsley and the optional almonds.

Broccoli, Apple, and Peanut Soup

Luscious and nutty, with a touch of sweetness

6 to 8 servings

Peanut butter gives this soup a rich flavor. In my home, this is a fall favorite!

1½ tablespoons olive oil

2 large onions, chopped

2 cloves garlic, minced

3 medium carrots, peeled and sliced

4 cups water with 2 vegetable bouillon cubes, or other stock option (page 9)

2 medium apples, peeled, cored, and diced

1 teaspoon good-quality curry powder

⅔ cup smooth or chunky natural peanut butter

6 heaping cups finely chopped broccoli florets and peeled stems

Juice of ½ lemon

Salt and freshly ground pepper to taste

Chopped roasted peanuts for garnish, optional

Per serving:
Calories: 250   Total fat: 16 g   Protein: 10 g   Fiber: 6 g
Carbohydrate: 22 g   Cholesterol: 0 mg   Sodium: 76 mg

Heat the oil in a soup pot. Add the onions and sauté over medium-low heat until translucent. Add the garlic and carrots and continue to sauté until the onions are golden.

Add the water with bouillon cubes, apples, and curry powder. Bring to a rapid simmer, then lower the heat. Cover and simmer gently for 10 to 15 minutes, or until the carrots and apple are tender. Remove from the heat.

Transfer the solid ingredients to a food processor with a slotted spoon. Process until just coarsely pureed, leaving plenty of chunks of carrot. Stir the puree back into the soup pot. Or insert an immersion blender into the pot and process until coarsely pureed.

Add the peanut butter to the soup, about half at a time, whisking in until completely blended with the stock. Return to very low heat.

Steam the broccoli in a saucepan with about ¼ cup water, covered, for 5 minutes, or until brightly colored and tender-crisp to your liking. Stir into the soup.

If the soup is too thick, add enough stock or water to achieve a medium-thick consistency. Add the lemon juice, then season with salt and pepper. Serve at once, passing around chopped peanuts for topping, if desired.

Swiss Chard Stew
with tortellini and sun-dried tomatoes

8 or more servings

Here's a bountiful and nourishing stew made substantial with the delightful addition of tortellini.

⅔ cup sun-dried tomatoes (not oil-cured)

1 tablespoon extra-virgin olive oil

1 medium onion, finely chopped

2 cloves garlic, minced

2 medium carrots, peeled and finely diced

1 large bunch Swiss chard (10 to 12 ounces)

4 cups water

One 16-ounce can salt-free diced tomatoes, undrained

One 10- to 12-ounce package frozen vegan tortellini (such as tofu- or spinach-filled), partially thawed

1½ teaspoons Italian herb seasoning

1 medium yellow summer squash, finely diced

2 tablespoons minced fresh dill, or 1 teaspoon dried

Salt and freshly ground pepper to taste

8 fresh basil leaves, thinly sliced

Per serving:
Calories: 115   Total fat: 4 g   Protein: 5 g   Fiber: 4 g
Carbohydrate: 17 g   Cholesterol: 0 mg   Sodium: 437 mg

Cover the dried tomatoes with about 1 cup boiling water in a small bowl. Let stand until needed.

Heat the oil in a large soup pot. Add the onion, garlic, and carrots and sauté over medium-low heat, stirring occasionally, until all are golden.

Meanwhile, rinse the chard well, trim away the thick midribs, and cut into approximately ½-by-2-inch shreds. Place in another large pot with just enough water to keep the bottom of the pot moist. Cover and cook until just tender and bright green, about 5 to 7 minutes. Remove from the heat and set aside until needed.

Add the water, tomatoes, tortellini, and seasoning to the soup pot. Bring to a rapid simmer, then lower the heat. Cover and simmer gently for 15 minutes, or until the carrots are just tender.

Add the squash and dill. Cover and simmer over low heat for another 10 minutes, or until the tortellini and the squash are done. Stir in the reserved chard, and add more water if needed to give the stew a moist yet not soupy consistency. Season with salt and pepper, then serve at once, garnishing each serving with a few strips of basil.

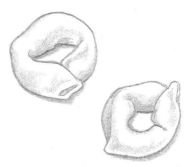

Sweet-and-Sauerkraut Soup

with tempeh or "sausage" topping

6 to 8 servings

This hearty sweet-and-sour soup takes the chill out of nippy fall afternoons. Serve with Onion-Rye Scones (page 155) or fresh rye bread.

3 tablespoons olive oil

1 large onion, quartered and thinly sliced

2 medium carrots, peeled and thinly sliced

1 large celery stalk, finely diced

4 cups water with 2 vegetable bouillon cubes, or other stock option (page 9)

3 medium Yukon Gold or red-skinned potatoes, peeled and diced

2 medium apples, peeled and diced

One 16-ounce can sauerkraut, well drained

One 16-ounce can salt-free diced tomatoes, undrained

1 teaspoon salt-free seasoning (see page 4 for brands)

One 16-ounce can small white beans, drained and rinsed

2 tablespoons natural granulated sugar, more or less to taste

Salt and freshly ground pepper to taste

One 8- to 12-ounce package tempeh, any variety, or one 8-ounce package soy sausage links

Per serving:
Calories: 317   Total fat: 9 g   Protein: 14 g   Fiber: 9 g
Carbohydrate: 48 g   Cholesterol: 0 mg   Sodium: 270 mg

Heat half of the oil in a soup pot. Add the onion, carrots, and celery and sauté over medium heat until all are golden.

Add the water with bouillon cubes and the potatoes. Bring to a rapid simmer, then lower the heat. Cover and simmer gently for 15 minutes, or until the potatoes are just tender.

Stir in the apples, sauerkraut, tomatoes, seasoning, and beans. Simmer for another 15 to 20 minutes, or until everything is tender.

Adjust the consistency with a bit more water if the soup seems crowded. Add sugar in small amounts to balance the tartness of the sauerkraut, tasting as you add. Season with salt and pepper (you may need very little salt, if any). If time allows, let the soup stand off the heat for an hour or so.

Just before serving, cut the tempeh into dice, or cut the soy sausage into ½-inch-thick slices. Heat the remaining oil in a medium skillet. Add the tempeh or sausage and sauté over medium-high heat, stirring frequently, until crisp and browned on most sides. Meanwhile, heat the soup through. Top each serving with some of the tempeh or sausage.

An idealist is one who, on noticing that a rose smells better than a cabbage, concludes that it will also make a better soup.

—H.L. Mencken (1880–1956)

Garlicky Cream of Celery Soup

A perfect puree for a rainy fall day

6 servings

This smooth soup will win you over with its elegant simplicity and intense celery flavor. Serve with Garlic Croutons (page 159).

12 large celery stalks
2 tablespoons olive oil
1 large onion, chopped
8 cloves garlic, minced
2 tablespoons unbleached white flour
3 medium potatoes, peeled and diced
2 teaspoons salt-free seasoning
　(see page 4 for brands)
⅓ cup mixed chopped fresh parsley and dill
Handful of celery leaves, chopped
1 to 1½ cups rice milk, as needed
¼ cup Silk creamer
Salt and freshly ground pepper to taste
Chopped fresh dill or parsley for garnish

Per serving:
Calories: 156　Total fat: 6 g　Protein: 3 g　Fiber: 3 g
Carbohydrate: 24 g　Cholesterol: 0 mg　Sodium: 87 mg

Last night with the celery, autumn came into its own. There is a crispness about celery that is the essence of October. It is as fresh and clean as a rainy day after a spell of heat.

—A.A. Milne
　Not That It Matters, 1920

Trim the bottoms off of the celery and remove the strings with a vegetable peeler. Cut 10 of the stalks into ½-inch slices. Cut the remaining 2 stalks into ¼-inch dice, and set aside.

Heat 1 tablespoon of the oil in a soup pot. Add the onion and garlic and sauté over medium heat until the onion is lightly golden.

Sprinkle in the flour and stir it in until it disappears. Add the sliced celery, the potatoes, and just enough water to cover. Bring to a rapid simmer, then lower the heat. Add the seasoning, fresh herbs, and celery leaves. Cover and simmer gently until the vegetables are tender, about 25 minutes. Remove from the heat.

With a slotted spoon, transfer the solid ingredients to a food processor or blender and puree, in batches if necessary, until smoothly pureed, then stir back into the soup pot. Or insert an immersion blender into the pot and puree the soup until smooth. Return to low heat and add enough rice milk to give the soup a slightly thick consistency. Stir in the creamer.

Heat the remaining oil in a small skillet. Add the reserved celery and sauté over medium heat until touched with golden spots. Stir into the soup, then season with salt and pepper. Serve at once, or allow the soup to stand off the heat for an hour or so, then heat through before serving. Garnish each serving with chopped dill or parsley.

Hot-and-Sour Asian Vegetable Soup

An extravaganza of invigorating textures and flavors

6 servings

Don't be intimidated by the long list of ingredients here. It's an easy soup to make, doesn't take long to cook, and is full of exciting textures and flavors. Thanks to Neil Trager, who gave me this recipe many moons ago.

6 dried shiitake mushrooms

1 tablespoon light olive or peanut oil

1 teaspoon dark sesame oil

1 medium onion, quartered and sliced

2 or 3 stalks bok choy or 2 large celery stalks,
    sliced diagonally

One 14- to 16-ounce can salt-free diced
    tomatoes, undrained

1 cup fresh white mushrooms,
    coarsely chopped

4 cups water

½ teaspoon black pepper or lemon pepper

1 cup snow peas, cut into 1-inch pieces

One 15-ounce can baby corn, undrained

3 to 5 tablespoons rice vinegar, to taste

Chili oil, cayenne pepper, or Asian hot sauce,
    to taste

2 tablespoons reduced-sodium soy sauce

8 ounces extra-firm tofu, cut into ½-inch dice

2 scallions, white and green parts, minced

2 tablespoons cornstarch

Per serving:
Calories: 134   Total fat: 6 g   Protein: 6 g   Fiber: 5 g
Carbohydrate: 18 g   Cholesterol: 0 mg   Sodium: 380 mg

Place the dried mushrooms in a bowl to soak with about 1 cup boiling water and set aside until needed.

Heat both oils in a soup pot. Add the onion and sauté over low heat until golden. Add the bok choy, tomatoes, white mushrooms, water, and pepper. Bring to a rapid simmer, then lower the heat. Cover and simmer gently until the bok choy is tender-crisp, about 5 minutes.

Meanwhile, trim and discard the tough stems of the soaked mushrooms, reserving the broth. Slice the caps. Add them with their broth to the soup.

Add the remaining ingredients except the cornstarch. Taste frequently as you add the vinegar and hot seasoning. Simmer over very low heat for 5 minutes longer.

Dissolve the cornstarch in ¼ cup water. Slowly drizzle into the soup while stirring. Simmer over very low heat for another 2 to 3 minutes. Remove from the heat and serve at once.

"Buddha's Delight" Stew

with seitan, green vegetables, and mushrooms

6 to 8 servings

*Inspired by a favorite vegetarian Chinese restau-
rant dish, this stew is enhanced with protein-
packed seitan. Made from cooked wheat gluten,
seitan is sometimes called "wheat meat," as it
resembles beef chunks. Though dense and chewy
and somewhat "meaty," seitan is low in fat,
quite high in protein, and its grainy flavor will
likely not put off those who don't care for meat.*

16 ounces seitan, broth reserved

1 large bunch broccoli, cut into
   bite-sized pieces

2 cups fresh green beans, trimmed and cut
   into 1-inch pieces

3 large carrots, peeled and sliced diagonally

2 cloves garlic, minced

4 ounces fine rice noodles

1 recipe Asian Mushroom Broth (page 15),
   with trimmed shiitake mushrooms,
   or one 32-ounce carton low-sodium
   vegetable broth

1½ cups crimini, baby bella, or small white
   mushrooms

One 15-ounce can baby corn, drained
   (reserve liquid for another use)

3 tablespoons cornstarch

3 tablespoons reduced-sodium soy sauce,
   or to taste

Per serving:
Calories: 256   Total fat: 3 g   Protein: 22 g   Fiber: 7 g
Carbohydrate: 38 g   Cholesterol: 0 mg   Sodium: 975 mg

Drain the broth from the seitan (you'll likely get ¾ to
1 cup) into a soup pot or large, steep-sided stir-fry pan.
Cut the seitan into bite-sized chunks and set aside. Add
the broccoli, green beans, carrots, and garlic. Bring to
a rapid simmer, then lower the heat. Cover and simmer
for 5 minutes, or until the broccoli and green beans are
bright green.

Cook the noodles according to package directions until
al dente, then drain and cut into shorter lengths. Set aside
until needed.

Meanwhile, add the broth with shiitake mushrooms,
seitan, white mushrooms, and baby corn to the stew.
Bring to a rapid simmer, then lower the heat. Cook over
medium-high heat, uncovered, until the vegetables are
tender-crisp, about 8 to 10 minutes.

Put the cornstarch in a small bowl or mixing cup and
stir in just enough of the liquid from the soup pot to
smoothly dissolve it. Slowly pour into the soup pot and
simmer just until the broth has thickened up. Stir in the
soy sauce and noodles, and serve at once.

African-Inspired Quinoa-Peanut Soup

A chunky feast of sweet potato, zucchini, and peppers in a nutty base

6 to 8 servings

This easy, robust soup, contributed by Marti Hall, has several elements of a certain style of traditional African soups—chilies, sweet potato, and a creamy peanut base. The grain of choice in an African soup like this would likely be millet, but here, quinoa, the nutritious South American super grain, makes for a delightful fusion.

2 tablespoons olive oil

1 large red onion, chopped

2 to 4 cloves garlic, minced

1 medium red bell pepper, diced

2 celery stalks, diced

1 fresh jalapeño, seeded and minced, or one 4-ounce can chopped mild green chilies

Handful of celery leaves, chopped

1 large sweet potato, peeled and diced

5 cups water with 2 vegetable bouillon cubes, or other stock option (page 9)

2 medium-small zucchini, diced

1 teaspoon ground cumin

1 teaspoon dried oregano

1 teaspoon grated fresh ginger

½ cup raw quinoa, rinsed

½ cup smooth or chunky natural peanut butter

Salt and freshly ground pepper to taste

Cayenne pepper or dried hot red pepper flakes, to taste

Per serving:
Calories: 242   Total fat: 14 g   Protein: 8 g   Fiber: 4 g
Carbohydrate: 24 g   Cholesterol: 0 mg   Sodium: 68 mg

Heat the oil in a soup pot. Sauté the onion over medium heat until translucent, then add the garlic, bell pepper, and celery. Sauté 10 to 15 minutes, or until the vegetables are golden and softened.

Add the remaining ingredients except the last three. Bring to a rapid simmer, then lower the heat. Cover and simmer gently until the quinoa is cooked and the vegetables are tender, about 15 minutes.

Add the peanut butter, stirring well to blend in completely, then simmer over very low heat for another 10 minutes, or until the quinoa is puffy and the sweet potato is tender.

Season with salt, pepper, and cayenne. If time allows, let the soup stand off the heat for an hour or so. It will thicken as it stands. Just before serving, adjust the consistency with water as needed, then heat through. Adjust the seasonings, then serve.

WINTER

Winter is the very best time for hearty soups and stews—nothing offers better comfort to body and spirit when coming in from the cold. What a perfect time to make thick soups of grains and legumes. Teamed with bread and salad, most of the soups in this section make satisfying meals in and of themselves.

Minestrone

An easy rendition of Italian vegetable soup

8 or more servings

Filling and flavorful, this becomes a meal in itself when served with a robust bread such as Focaccia Bread (page 148). It keeps exceptionally well and develops flavor as it stands.

2 tablespoons extra-virgin olive oil

2 medium onions, finely chopped

2 cloves garlic, minced

2 medium carrots, peeled and diced

2 medium celery stalks, diced

Handful of celery leaves, chopped

2 medium potatoes, peeled and diced

One 16-ounce can salt-free diced tomatoes, undrained

1 cup salt-free tomato sauce

¼ cup dry red wine, optional

2 bay leaves

2 teaspoons Italian herb seasoning

1 cup canned chickpeas, drained and rinsed

1 cup frozen green peas, thawed

2 tablespoons minced fresh parsley

Salt and freshly ground pepper to taste

Per serving:
Calories: 130   Total fat: 3 g   Protein: 5 g   Fiber: 6 g
Carbohydrate: 24 g   Cholesterol: 0 mg   Sodium: 190 mg

Heat the oil in a soup pot. Add the onions and sauté over medium-low heat until translucent. Add the garlic and continue to sauté until both are golden.

Add the carrots, celery and leaves, and potatoes, along with just enough water to cover. Stir in the tomatoes, tomato sauce, optional wine, bay leaves, and seasoning. Bring to a rapid simmer, then lower the heat. Cover and simmer gently until the vegetables are just done, about 20 to 25 minutes.

Add the chickpeas, green peas, and parsley. Adjust the consistency with more water as needed if the soup is too crowded, then season with salt and pepper.

Simmer over low heat for at least another 20 to 30 minutes, or until the vegetables are completely tender, but not overdone. Discard the bay leaves and serve.

Italian Pasta and Bean Soup

The classic *pasta e fagiole*, with lots of zucchini

8 or more servings

Like minestrone, this is an Italian standard. Serve it with Bruschetta (page 159) or fresh garlic bread.

2 tablespoons extra-virgin olive oil

1 medium onion, finely chopped

2 cloves garlic, minced

1 medium carrot, peeled and cut into
   ¼-inch dice

1 large celery stalk, cut into ¼-inch dice

4 cups cooked cannellini beans (about
   1½ cups dried), or two 16-ounce cans,
   drained and rinsed

6 cups cooking liquid from beans, or 6 cups
   water with 2 vegetable bouillon cubes

2 cups diced zucchini

2 bay leaves

1½ teaspoons Italian herb seasoning

¼ cup salt-free tomato paste

1½ cups ditalini (tiny tubular pasta)

2 tablespoons chopped fresh parsley

Salt and freshly ground pepper to taste

Per serving:
Calories: 224   Total fat: 5 g   Protein: 12 g   Fiber: 8 g
Carbohydrate: 36 g   Cholesterol: 0 mg   Sodium: 62 mg

Heat the oil in a soup pot. Add the onion, garlic, carrot, and celery and sauté over medium-low heat, stirring frequently, until golden.

Add the beans, cooking liquid, zucchini, bay leaves, seasoning, and tomato paste. Bring to a rapid simmer. Lower the heat, cover, and simmer gently until the zucchini is just tender, about 10 minutes. Remove from the heat and allow the soup to stand for an hour or so to develop flavor. Remove and discard the bay leaves.

Just before serving, cook the pasta until *al dente* in a separate saucepan. Drain and rinse briefly under cool water until it stops steaming. Stir into the soup along with the parsley. Season with salt and pepper and serve.

The making of a good soup is quite an art, and many otherwise clever cooks do not possess the tour de main necessary to its successful preparation. Either they overcomplicate the composition of the dish, or they attach only minor importance to it, reserving their talents for the meal itself, and so it frequently happens that the soup does not correspond to the quality of the rest of the dishes; nevertheless, the quality of the soup should foretell that of the entire meal.

—Madame Seignobos
   Comment on Forme une Cuisinière, 1903

Italian Mixed Vegetable Stew
with hearty potato gnocchi

8 or more servings

Gnocchi are dumplings made of semolina and potato flours. They add substance to this flavorful stew. At many supermarkets, you'll find them in the frozen food section near ravioli, tortellini, and other such Italian specialties. Serve with Bruschetta (page 159) and a green salad featuring olives and chickpeas.

2 tablespoons extra-virgin olive oil

1 large onion, chopped

3 cloves garlic, minced

2 medium potatoes, peeled and diced

One 10-ounce package frozen cut green beans

One 28-ounce can salt-free diced tomatoes, undrained

¼ cup dry red wine

1 teaspoon Italian herb seasoning

½ teaspoon dried basil

2 cups water

3 heaping cups cauliflower, cut into bite-sized pieces

1 medium zucchini, quartered lengthwise and sliced

1 pound frozen gnocchi, thawed

Salt and freshly ground pepper to taste

¼ cup chopped fresh parsley, or more to taste

Per serving:
Calories: 210   Total fat: 8 g   Protein: 6 g   Fiber: 6 g
Carbohydrate: 31 g   Cholesterol: 0 mg   Sodium: 88 mg

Heat the oil in a soup pot. Add the onion and sauté over medium-low heat until translucent. Add the garlic and continue to sauté until both are golden.

Add the potatoes, green beans, tomatoes, wine, seasoning, and basil. Stir in the water. Bring to a rapid simmer. Lower the heat, cover, and simmer gently until the vegetables are just tender, about 15 minutes.

Add the cauliflower and zucchini and cook for another 10 to 15 minutes, or until all the vegetables are done but not overcooked.

Meanwhile, cook the gnocchi separately in a large pot according to package directions. Most prepared gnocchi cook in about 10 minutes. When done, drain and gently stir into the stew.

Season with salt and pepper and stir in half of the parsley. The stew should have a thick, moist base, but not be too liquidy. Add a bit more water if needed.

Serve at once. Top each serving with a sprinkling of the remaining parsley.

Macaroni and Cheese Soup

A comforting bowl of pasta and cheese in a base of pureed white beans

6 to 8 servings

Here's a favorite nursery food converted into a mild, high-protein soup.

1½ tablespoons nonhydrogenated
    margarine or olive oil
1 large onion, finely chopped
2 medium celery stalks, finely diced
Two 16-ounce cans cannellini beans,
    drained and rinsed
2 cups water
1 vegetable bouillon cube
1½ teaspoons salt-free seasoning
    (see page 4 for brands)
1 teaspoon dry mustard
½ teaspoon dried dill
1½ to 2 cups rice milk, or as needed
1½ cups firmly packed cheddar-style
    nondairy cheese
1 cup frozen green peas
2 cups small pasta, such as tiny shells
    or elbows
Salt and freshly ground pepper to taste

Per serving:
Calories: 333   Total fat: 10 g   Protein: 11 g   Fiber: 9 g
Carbohydrate: 50 g   Cholesterol: 0 mg   Sodium: 460 mg

Heat the margarine in a soup pot. Add the onion and celery and sauté over medium-low heat until both are golden.

Meanwhile, puree the beans in a blender or food processor until smooth. Add a small amount of water if necessary.

Cover the onions and celery with 2 cups water. Stir in the bean puree, bouillon cube, and seasonings. Bring to a rapid simmer, then lower the heat. Cover and simmer gently for 20 to 25 minutes.

Stir in enough rice milk to give the soup a slightly thick consistency. Bring the soup to a gentle simmer once again. Sprinkle in the cheese, a bit at a time, stirring in each time until fairly well melted. Add the peas and continue to cook over very low heat.

In a separate saucepan, cook the pasta until *al dente*. Drain well and stir into the soup. Adjust the consistency of the soup with more rice milk, if needed, then season with salt and pepper and serve.

Mock Chicken Noodle Soup

Quite unlike the kind my mom made

6 servings

This simple, soothing soup recalls a comfort soup from my childhood. It proves that winter soups need not always be thick to provide a sense of warmth. I like to use a mild-flavored variety of baked tofu in this, such as Soy Boy Tofu Lin.

1 tablespoon olive oil

2 large celery stalks, finely diced

3 medium carrots, peeled and thinly sliced

2 to 3 cloves garlic, minced

1 small onion, minced

6 cups water with 2 vegetable bouillon cubes,
   or other stock option (page 9)

1 teaspoon salt-free seasoning
   (see page 4 for brands)

½ teaspoon dried dill

4 to 6 ounces short, fine noodles (see Note)

4 to 6 ounces baked tofu, finely diced

Salt and freshly ground pepper to taste

Per serving:
Calories: 157   Total fat: 5 g   Protein: 7 g   Fiber: 2 g
Carbohydrate: 21 g   Cholesterol: 0 mg   Sodium: 163 mg

Heat the oil in a large soup pot. Add the celery, carrots, garlic, onion, and about 2 tablespoons water. Cover and sweat over medium heat for about 10 minutes, or until the vegetables begin to soften.

Add the water with bouillon cubes, seasoning, and dried dill. Bring to a rapid simmer. Lower the heat, cover, and simmer gently for 15 minutes, or until the vegetables are tender.

Raise the heat and bring to a more vigorous simmer. Add the noodles and simmer steadily for 5 to 8 minutes, or until *al dente*.

Stir in the diced tofu, then season with salt and pepper. Serve at once. As the soup stands, the noodles quickly absorb the liquid. If you plan on having leftovers of the soup, add a cup or so of additional water before storing, and adjust the seasonings. This way the soup can develop more flavor as it stands.

NOTE:

You can use vermicelli or angel hair, broken into 1½-inch pieces; soba noodles are good too, if you want something a bit more nourishing or assertive. Fine, round noodles such as anellini are also good.

Potato Soup with Pink and Green Beans

A warming soup featuring the fresh taste of dill

6 servings

Both soothing and lively, thanks to the flavor of dill, this simple soup is one of my cold-weather favorites.

1 tablespoon olive oil

1 medium onion, finely chopped

2 cloves garlic, minced

4 medium potatoes, scrubbed and diced

One 28-ounce can salt-free diced or
   stewed tomatoes

¼ cup dry white wine

1 teaspoon ground cumin

1 teaspoon paprika

1 teaspoon salt-free seasoning (see page 4
   for brands)

One 16-ounce can pink beans, drained
   and rinsed

2 cups frozen cut green beans, thawed

2 tablespoons minced fresh dill

¼ cup chopped fresh parsley

Salt and freshly ground pepper to taste

Per serving:
Calories: 212   Total fat: 3 g   Protein: 9 g   Fiber: 9 g
Carbohydrate: 41 g   Cholesterol: 0 mg   Sodium: 168 mg

Heat the oil in a soup pot. Add the onion and sauté over medium-low heat until translucent. Add the garlic and continue to sauté until both are golden.

Add the potatoes with just enough water to cover, followed by the tomatoes (if using stewed tomatoes, chop them before adding), wine, and spices. Bring to a rapid simmer, then lower the heat. Cover and simmer gently for 20 minutes.

Stir in the pink beans and green beans. Cover and simmer gently for 15 to 20 minutes longer.

Stir in the dill and parsley, then season with salt and pepper. Serve at once, or if time allows, let the soup stand off the heat for an hour or two, then heat through before serving.

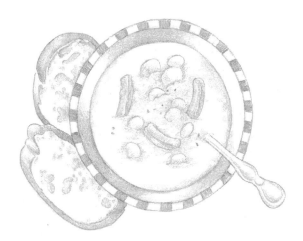

Winter Celery, Potato, and Mushroom Soup

An everyday soup featuring winter vegetables and a bit of barley

6 servings

This is just the sort of mild soup that is so comforting on cold winter days. Quick Sunflower-Cheese Bread (page 144) is a good accompaniment, as are Cheddar-Oat Griddle Biscuits (page 153).

2 tablespoons olive oil

1 large onion, chopped

2 tablespoons unbleached white flour

5 cups water with 2 vegetable bouillon cubes,
    or other stock option (page 9)

4 large celery stalks, diced

Handful of celery leaves, chopped

3 medium potatoes, diced

⅓ cup raw pearl or pot barley, rinsed

2 bay leaves

½ pound mushrooms, coarsely chopped

2 teaspoons salt-free seasoning
    (see page 4 for brands)

1 cup frozen green peas, thawed

1½ to 2 cups rice milk, or as needed

Salt and freshly ground pepper to taste

Per serving:

Calories: 259   Total fat: 8 g   Protein: 5 g   Fiber: 8 g
Carbohydrate: 49 g   Cholesterol: 0 mg   Sodium: 97 mg

Heat the oil in a soup pot. Add the onion and sauté over medium-low heat until golden.

Sprinkle in the flour a bit at a time and stir in. Slowly stir in about 1 cup of the water, then add the remaining water with bouillon cubes, celery, celery leaves, potatoes, barley, and bay leaves. Bring to a rapid simmer, then lower the heat. Cover and simmer gently for 15 minutes.

Add the mushrooms and seasoning, and simmer until the barley is tender, about 25 to 30 minutes longer. Add the peas and enough rice milk to give the soup a medium-thick consistency.

Season with salt and pepper, and simmer over very low heat for another 10 minutes. Discard the bay leaves. This soup thickens as it stands; thin any leftovers with additional water or rice milk, then taste to adjust the seasonings.

Creamy Parsnip-Vegetable Soup

A trio of root vegetables in a creamy base

... mild soup for cold ... with Garlic Croutons

... and cut into

... peeled and cut into
  ½-inch dice
2 medium carrots, peeled and coarsely
  chopped
One 16-ounce can salt-free diced tomatoes,
  undrained
1½ teaspoons salt-free seasoning (see page 4
  for brands)
2 vegetable bouillon cubes
2 tablespoons minced fresh parsley
1½ cups rice milk, or as needed
½ cup Silk creamer
Salt and freshly ground pepper to taste

Per serving:
Calories: 259   Total fat: 8 g   Protein: 5 g   Fiber: 8 g
Carbohydrate: 49 g   Cholesterol: 0 mg   Sodium: 97 mg

Heat the oil in a soup pot. Add the onion and celery and sauté over medium-low heat until both are golden.

Add the celery leaves, parsnips, potatoes, carrots, tomatoes, seasoning, bouillon cubes, and just enough water to barely cover the vegetables. Bring to a rapid simmer, then lower the heat. Cover and simmer gently until the vegetables are tender, about 20 to 30 minutes. Remove from the heat.

With a slotted spoon, transfer half of the vegetables to a food processor or blender. Process until smoothly pureed, then stir back into the soup. Or simply insert an immersion blender into the soup pot and process until about half of the soup is pureed.

Stir in the parsley and enough rice milk to give the soup a slightly thick consistency. Stir in the creamer, then season with salt and pepper. Return the soup to low heat and simmer very gently for 10 to 15 minutes.

Serve at once, or if time allows, let the soup stand off the heat for an hour or so, then heat through before serving. This soup thickens as it cools. Thin the consistency of any leftover soup with additional rice milk, and adjust the seasonings.

Parsnip dressed in creame ... will fatten exceedingly; but it ingenders lust and longing desires.

—William Vaughn
  Directions for Health, 1600

Hearty Winter Roots Soup

A chunky mélange of rutabaga, carrots, potatoes, and parsnips
with a hint of cheese

6 to 8 servings

*This hearty soup makes use of a couple of
underused winter vegetables—parsnips and
rutabaga—to great results. Make sure you have
a good, sharp knife for cutting the rutabaga.*

2 tablespoons olive oil

1 large onion, chopped

2 cups peeled, diced rutabaga

2 medium carrots, peeled and coarsely
    chopped

2 medium potatoes, scrubbed and diced

2 medium parsnips, scraped and diced

1 large celery stalk, diced

⅓ cup quick-cooking oats

¼ cup dry white wine

2 teaspoons salt-free seasoning
    (see page 4 for brands)

2 vegetable bouillon cubes

1 cup rice milk, or as needed

¼ cup Silk creamer

1 cup grated cheddar-style nondairy cheese

Salt and freshly ground pepper to taste

Per serving:
Calories: 212   Total fat: 9 g   Protein: 4 g   Fiber: 6 g
Carbohydrate: 32 g   Cholesterol: 0 mg   Sodium: 140 mg

Heat the oil in a soup pot. Add the onion and sauté over
medium heat until golden.

Add the rutabaga, carrots, potatoes, parsnips, celery,
oats, wine, seasoning, bouillon cubes, and just enough
water to barely cover the vegetables. Bring to a rapid
simmer, then lower the heat. Cover and simmer gently
until the vegetables are tender, about 25 to 30 minutes.

With a slotted spoon, remove about 2 cups of the
vegetables and transfer to a shallow bowl or a plate.
Mash coarsely, then stir back into the soup. Add the rice
milk and allow the soup to simmer over very low heat for
another 10 minutes.

Stir in the creamer, then sprinkle in the cheese, a little at
a time, stirring in until fairly well melted each time.

If the soup is too thick, adjust the consistency with a bit
more rice milk. Season with salt and pepper. Serve at
once, or if time allows, let the soup stand off the heat for
an hour or so before serving, then heat through gently
before serving.

Baby Carrot Bisque

A puree of carrots and tomatoes in a creamy tofu base

6 to 8 servings

The sweetness of baby carrots and a pretty, pale-orange color make this an uplifting dish for a chilly winter day.

2 tablespoons olive oil

1 large onion, chopped

One 16-ounce bag baby carrots

2 medium turnips, peeled and diced

2 bay leaves

2 teaspoons salt-free seasoning (see page 4 for brands)

One 12.3-ounce package firm silken tofu, crumbled

One 16-ounce can salt-free diced tomatoes, undrained

1 teaspoon grated fresh ginger

¼ teaspoon cinnamon

3 scallions, sliced

1 cup frozen green peas, thawed

2 to 3 tablespoons finely chopped fresh parsley

½ cup orange juice, freshly squeezed or store-bought organic

Salt and freshly ground pepper to taste

Per serving:
Calories: 144   Total fat: 6 g   Protein: 5 g   Fiber: 4 g
Carbohydrate: 19 g   Cholesterol: 0 mg   Sodium: 80 mg

Heat 1 tablespoon of the oil in a large soup pot. Add the onion and sauté over medium-low heat until golden.

Add the carrots, half of the diced turnips (set aside the rest), bay leaves, and seasoning. Add just enough water to barely cover the vegetables. Bring to a rapid simmer, then lower the heat. Cover and simmer gently for 25 to 30 minutes, or until the vegetables are tender.

Remove from the heat. Discard the bay leaves. With a slotted spoon, transfer the vegetables to a food processor or blender. Process until smoothly pureed, then transfer back to the soup pot.

Combine the tofu and tomatoes in the food processor or blender. Process until smoothly pureed and transfer to the soup pot. Stir until both purees are well integrated, and return to medium heat. Stir in the ginger and cinnamon.

Heat the remaining tablespoon of oil in a small skillet. Add the reserved turnip dice and sauté over medium heat until tender-crisp and golden, stirring frequently. Add the scallions and sauté another minute or so, until just wilted. Remove from the heat and stir the mixture into the soup.

Stir in the peas, parsley, and orange juice. Season with salt and pepper. The soup should have a smooth, medium-thick consistency. Add a bit more juice or water if necessary.

Simmer very gently over low heat for 5 to 10 minutes longer. If time allows, let the soup stand off the heat for an hour or two, then heat through before serving.

Sweet-and-Sour Cabbage and Bread Stew

A hearty bowlful of cold-weather comfort

6 servings

Here's a variation of classic sweet-and-sour cab-bage soup, given a bit more heft with bread cubes nestled in each serving.

3 to 4 cups cubed (about 1 inch) Italian or
   sourdough bread
2 tablespoons olive oil
2 large onions, quartered and thinly sliced
3 to 4 cloves garlic, minced
5 cups water
2 large carrots, peeled and diced
2 large or 3 medium potatoes, diced
4 cups coarsely shredded green cabbage
1 medium green or red bell pepper, diced
One 16-ounce can salt-free diced or stewed
   tomatoes, undrained
¼ cup dry red wine
1 teaspoon paprika
½ teaspoon ground cumin
3 tablespoons lemon juice, or to taste
3 tablespoons natural granulated sugar
Salt and freshly ground pepper to taste

Per serving:
Calories: 231   Total fat: 6 g   Protein: 6 g   Fiber: 6 g
Carbohydrate: 43 g   Cholesterol: 0 mg   Sodium: 114 mg

Preheat the oven to 300 degrees. Spread the bread cubes in a single layer on a baking sheet and bake until golden and crisp, about 12 to 15 minutes. Remove from the oven and set aside.

Heat the oil in a large soup pot. Add the onions and garlic and sauté over medium heat until golden, about 10 minutes.

Add the water, carrots, potatoes, cabbage, bell pepper, tomatoes, wine, paprika, and cumin. Bring to a rapid simmer, then lower the heat. Cover and simmer gently for 30 to 35 minutes, or until the vegetables are tender.

Stir in the lemon juice and sugar. There should be a subtle sweet-sour balance. If you'd like it to be more pronounced, add more lemon juice and/or sugar to your liking.

Season with salt and pepper, then simmer over very low heat for 10 minutes longer. If time allows, let the stew stand off the heat for an hour or two, then heat through before serving.

When ready to serve, divide the bread cubes among the serving bowls and ladle the stew over them. The bread will absorb much of the liquid and add a tasty, textural element to the stew.

Having a good wife and rich cabbage soup, seek not other things.

—Russian proverb

Spanish Garbanzo Stew

A slew of chickpeas, well flavored with tomatoes, garlic, and parsley

6 to 8 servings

This classic recipe is easy and quick to prepare. Serve with Tomato-Olive Bread (page 147) and a simple homemade coleslaw.

1½ tablespoons extra-virgin olive oil

1 large onion, chopped

3 to 4 cloves garlic, minced

1 large green bell pepper, cut into short, narrow strips

2 cups water

Two 16-ounce cans chickpeas, drained and rinsed

One 28-ounce can salt-free diced tomatoes, undrained

1 teaspoon ground cumin

1 teaspoon dried oregano

¼ teaspoon dried thyme

2 to 3 tablespoons chopped fresh parsley

Salt and freshly ground pepper to taste

Hot cooked rice, optional

Per serving:
Calories: 186   Total fat: 6 g   Protein: 7 g   Fiber: 9 g
Carbohydrate: 29 g   Cholesterol: 0 mg   Sodium: 200 mg

Heat the oil in a large soup pot. Add the onion and sauté over medium-low heat until translucent. Add the garlic and green pepper and continue to sauté until all are golden.

Add the water, chickpeas, tomatoes, cumin, oregano, and thyme. Bring to a rapid simmer, then lower the heat. Cover and simmer gently for 20 minutes.

Stir in the parsley and season sparingly with salt and generously with pepper. Adjust the consistency with more water as needed, but let the stew remain thick. Serve over a small amount of hot cooked rice, if desired.

Chickpea and Bulgur Stew
A tasty grain-and-bean combo with celery, turnips, and cabbage

6 to 8 servings

Bulgur is not often used in soups, but works very nicely, adding protein and a chewy texture.

2½ tablespoons olive oil

1 large onion, chopped

2 to 3 cloves garlic, minced

2 large celery stalks, diced

4 cups water

2 medium white turnips, peeled and diced

½ cup finely shredded cabbage

½ cup raw bulgur

One 28-ounce can salt-free diced
    tomatoes, undrained

2 bay leaves

2 teaspoons Italian herb seasoning

1 teaspoon paprika

One 16-ounce can chickpeas, drained and
    rinsed

Salt and freshly ground pepper to taste

1 medium green bell pepper, cut into short,
    narrow strips

Per serving:
Calories: 189   Total fat: 7 g   Protein: 6 g   Fiber: 8 g
Carbohydrate: 29 g   Cholesterol: 0 mg   Sodium: 150 mg

Heat 1½ tablespoons of the oil in a large soup pot. Add the onion and sauté over medium-low heat until translucent. Add the garlic and celery and continue to sauté until all are golden.

Add the water, turnips, cabbage, bulgur, tomatoes, bay leaves, seasoning, and paprika. Bring to a rapid simmer, then lower the heat. Cover and simmer gently for about 30 to 35 minutes, or until the bulgur and vegetables are tender. Discard the bay leaves.

Add the chickpeas, then season with salt and pepper. Simmer over very low heat for 10 minutes longer. If time allows, let the soup stand off the heat for about an hour, then heat through before serving.

Just before serving, heat the remaining oil in a small skillet. Sauté the bell pepper over medium heat until lightly touched with brown spots. After ladling the soup into bowls, top each serving with a few strips of sautéed bell pepper.

Golden Curried Pea Soup

The stick-to-your-ribs classic, gently spiced

8 or more servings

This long-simmering, yet easy winter soup is a natural choice as a hearty main dish. Make Whole Wheat Vegetable Muffins (page 149) while it's cooking.

2 tablespoons olive oil

1 cup finely chopped onion

2 medium carrots, peeled and diced

2 to 3 cloves garlic, crushed or minced

8 cups water

2 vegetable bouillon cubes

1 pound dried yellow split peas, rinsed

⅓ cup raw brown rice or barley, rinsed

2 bay leaves

2 teaspoons good-quality curry powder, more or less to taste

½ teaspoon turmeric

1 teaspoon grated fresh ginger

Pinch of ground nutmeg

Salt and freshly ground pepper to taste

Per serving:
Calories: 292   Total fat: 4 g   Protein: 17 g   Fiber: 1 g
Carbohydrate: 48 g   Cholesterol: 0 mg   Sodium: 47 mg

Heat the oil in a soup pot. Add the onion and sauté over medium-low heat until golden.

Add all the remaining ingredients except the salt and pepper. Bring to a rapid simmer, then lower the heat. Cover and simmer gently until the peas are mushy, about 1½ hours, stirring occasionally.

When the peas are done, adjust the consistency with more water as needed, then season with salt and pepper. Discard the bay leaves and serve. This soup thickens considerably as it stands; thin with additional water as needed and adjust the seasonings.

To ensure a good crop, plant peas when the moon is waning, so that they may grow as it does, and thus bear plentifully.

—Old European folk belief

Curried Millet-Spinach Soup

A medley of vegetables and greens with a hearty grain

8 servings

Millet, an exceptionally nutritious if rather bland grain, is used to great advantage in this soup, where it has an opportunity to soak up all the spicy flavors.

2 tablespoons olive oil

1 cup chopped onion

2 cloves garlic, minced

6 cups water

¾ cup raw millet, rinsed

2 medium potatoes, scrubbed and diced

1 large carrot, peeled and coarsely chopped

One 16-ounce can salt-free diced tomatoes,
   undrained

1 teaspoon grated fresh ginger

2 teaspoons good-quality curry powder

¼ teaspoon cinnamon

One 10-ounce package frozen chopped
   spinach, thawed

2 tablespoons finely chopped fresh parsley

Juice of ½ to 1 lemon, to taste

Salt and freshly ground pepper to taste

Per serving:

Calories: 158   Total fat: 4 g   Protein: 5 g   Fiber: 4 g
Carbohydrate: 27 g   Cholesterol: 0 mg   Sodium: 50 mg

Heat the oil in a soup pot. Add the onion and sauté over medium-low heat until translucent. Add the garlic and continue to sauté until both are golden.

Add the water, millet, potatoes, carrot, tomatoes, ginger, curry powder, and cinnamon. Bring to a rapid simmer, then lower the heat. Cover and simmer gently for 1 hour, or until the millet and vegetables are tender. Stir every 15 minutes or so.

Stir in the spinach, parsley, and lemon juice. If the soup is too thick, add a bit more water. Season with salt and pepper and simmer over very low heat for another 10 to 15 minutes, then serve.

This soup thickens as it stands, especially after refrigeration. Adjust the consistency with water as needed, then adjust the seasonings.

Brazilian Black Bean Stew

A beautiful bowl of black beans, sweet potatoes, and peppers served over rice

6 to 8 servings

A vegetarian version of Brazil's famous national dish, feijoada, this stew is abundant with nourishing ingredients. Serve with steamed fresh greens (you can dress them with garlic sautéed in olive oil) and slices of mango and/or papaya.

1 cup salt-free tomato juice

4½ cups water

1½ cups raw brown rice, rinsed

1 tablespoon olive oil

1 large onion, chopped

2 cloves garlic, minced

2 medium sweet potatoes, peeled and diced

4 cups cooked black beans (about 1⅔ cups dried), or two 16-ounce cans, drained and rinsed

1 medium red bell pepper, cut into short, narrow strips

1 medium green or yellow bell pepper, cut into short, narrow strips

1 cup diced ripe tomatoes, or 1 cup salt-free canned diced tomatoes

1 small fresh hot green chili, or more to taste

1½ teaspoons ground cumin

½ teaspoon dried thyme

½ cup chopped fresh parsley or cilantro

Salt and freshly ground pepper to taste

Per serving:
Calories: 363   Total fat: 4 g   Protein: 14 g   Fiber: 13 g
Carbohydrate: 71 g   Cholesterol: 0 mg   Sodium: 150 mg

Combine the tomato juice with 3 cups of the water in a large saucepan and bring to a simmer. Add the rice, then lower the heat and simmer gently, covered, until all the liquid is absorbed, about 30 minutes. Set aside.

Meanwhile, heat the oil in a large soup pot. Add the onion and sauté over medium-low heat until translucent. Add the garlic and continue to sauté until the onion is golden.

Stir in the sweet potatoes and the remaining 1½ cups of water. Bring to a rapid simmer, then lower the heat. Cover and simmer gently until the sweet potatoes are just tender but still firm, about 10 to 15 minutes.

Add the beans, bell peppers, tomatoes, chili, cumin, and thyme. Simmer gently for 10 to 15 minutes longer, uncovered. The stew should have the consistency of a thick chili—moist but not soupy. Add a bit more water if too thick.

Stir in half of the parsley and season with salt and pepper. Serve over the hot cooked rice in shallow bowls and garnish each serving with a little of the extra parsley.

Provençal Bean Pot
A wine-scented stew of small white beans

6 servings

This meatless version of a rustic Provençal stew is sensual and satisfying. A fresh, crusty French baguette is perfect for soaking up its delicious broth. A bountiful tossed salad makes it a complete meal.

2 tablespoons olive oil

1 large onion, chopped

3 to 4 cloves garlic, minced

2 cups water

2 medium carrots, peeled and sliced

4 celery stalks, diced

½ cup dry red wine

4 cups cooked navy beans (about 1⅔ cups dried), or two 16-ounce cans, drained and rinsed

One 16-ounce can salt-free diced tomatoes, undrained

½ teaspoon dried thyme

½ teaspoon minced fresh rosemary, or more to taste (or use ¼ to ½ teaspoon dried rosemary, to taste)

½ cup chopped fresh parsley

Salt and freshly ground pepper to taste

Per serving:
Calories: 270   Total fat: 5 g   Protein: 12 g   Fiber: 10 g
Carbohydrate: 42 g   Cholesterol: 0 mg   Sodium: 48 mg

Heat the oil in a soup pot. Add the onion and sauté until translucent. Add the garlic and continue to sauté over medium heat until both are golden.

Add the water, carrots, celery, and wine. Bring to a simmer, then cover and simmer gently for 10 minutes.

Stir in the beans, tomatoes, thyme, and rosemary. Bring to a simmer and cook over medium heat, covered, for 15 to 20 minutes. If needed, add a small amount of water, but the consistency should be neither too thick nor too soupy.

Stir in half of the parsley. Season with salt and pepper and serve. Sprinkle the remaining parsley atop each serving.

VARIATION:

To make this an even heartier dish, add some soy "sausage." Simply slice 4 to 6 links into ½-inch-thick slices, and sauté in a small amount of olive oil until golden brown on most sides. Stir into the stew once it's done, or pass around the sautéed soy sausage for those who would like to add some to their stew.

Spicy Chili Bean Stew

A vegan favorite—long simmering and well seasoned

8 or more servings

For those who like hot stuff, the hot chilies add a fiery kick to this soup. If you'd like a toned-down version, use mild chilies. This makes a big pot of soup, perfect for feeding a crowd. This is delicious served with a big salad and nachos or quesadillas made with Vegan Gourmet nacho-style nondairy cheese.

1 pound dried kidney, red, or pink beans, rinsed and sorted

2 tablespoons olive oil

1 large onion, chopped

2 to 3 cloves garlic, minced

2 bay leaves

One 16-ounce can salt-free diced tomatoes, undrained

¾ cup salt-free tomato sauce

2 teaspoons chili powder, more or less to taste

2 teaspoons ground cumin

2 fresh hot green chilies, seeded and minced

¼ cup raw bulgur, optional

1 cup frozen corn kernels , thawed

Salt to taste

1 large green bell pepper, cut into short, narrow strips

Chopped fresh cilantro for topping, optional

Per serving:

Calories: 292 Total fat: 4 g Protein: 16 g Fiber: 18 g

Carbohydrate: 51 g Cholesterol: 0 mg Sodium: 100 mg

Soak the beans overnight in plenty of water in a large covered soup pot. Or for a quicker soaking, cover the beans with water 2 hours or so before you begin the soup, bring to a boil, then cover and let stand off the heat. Once you're ready to begin the soup, drain the beans in a colander.

Heat 1 tablespoon of the oil in the same pot. Add the onion and sauté over medium-low heat until translucent. Add the garlic and continue to sauté until both are golden.

Return the beans to the pot with the onion and garlic. Cover with fresh water in a ratio of about double the water to the volume of beans. Bring to a rapid simmer, then lower the heat. Cover and simmer gently but steadily for 1 to 1½ hours, or until the beans are tender.

Add the bay leaves, tomatoes, tomato sauce, chili powder, cumin, chilies, and optional bulgur. Return to a simmer, then simmer gently over low heat for 30 minutes. Taste to make sure that the bulgur is tender; if not, simmer for 5 to 10 minutes more. Adjust the consistency with additional water if needed, but let the soup remain thick. Stir in the corn kernels and season with salt. Continue to simmer over very low heat.

Heat the remaining tablespoon of oil in a small skillet. Add the green bell pepper and sauté over medium heat, stirring frequently, until it is fragrant and just lightly touched with brown. Remove from the heat. Discard the bay leaves from the soup, then serve. Top each serving with a few strips of sautéed bell peppers and a sprinkling of cilantro, if desired.

White Bean and Hominy Chili

A colorful chili featuring whole hominy and sweet potatoes

6 to 8 servings

This offbeat chili is a pleasant introduction to whole hominy, if you've never tried it before. You'll find hominy near other canned corn products on supermarket shelves.

1 tablespoon olive oil

1 large onion, chopped

2 cloves garlic, minced

1 medium red or green bell pepper, cut into short, narrow strips

2 medium sweet potatoes, peeled and diced

2 cups water

One 16-ounce can great northern beans, drained and rinsed

One 16-ounce can whole white hominy

One 16-ounce can salt-free diced tomatoes, undrained

1 cup frozen corn kernels, thawed

One 4-ounce can chopped mild green chilies, or 1 to 2 chopped canned chipotle chilies in adobo, more or less to taste (see Note)

2 teaspoons ground cumin

1 teaspoon dried oregano

¼ cup chopped fresh cilantro or parsley

Salt to taste

Dried hot red pepper flakes to taste, optional

Per serving:
Calories: 228   Total fat: 3 g   Protein: 8 g   Fiber: 9 g
Carbohydrate: 44 g   Cholesterol: 0 mg   Sodium: 222 mg

Heat the oil in a large soup pot. Add the onion and sauté over medium-low heat until translucent. Add the garlic and continue to sauté until the onion is golden.

Stir in the bell pepper, sweet potatoes, and water. Bring to a rapid simmer, then lower the heat. Cover and simmer gently until the sweet potatoes are just tender but still firm, about 10 to 15 minutes.

Add the beans, hominy, tomatoes, corn, chilies, cumin, and oregano. Simmer gently for 20 to 25 minutes longer. Stir in the cilantro, and taste first before adding any salt. You may not need any due to the canned beans and hominy. If desired, season with red pepper flakes if you are not using chipotles.

The stew should have the consistency of a thick chili—moist, but not soupy. Add a bit more water if too thick. Serve at once, or let stand off the heat for an hour or so, then heat through before serving.

NOTE:
Using chipotle chilies will give this stew a smoky flavor, and will be spicier than if using mild green chilies.

If pale beans bubble for you in a red earthenware pot, you can often decline the dinners of sumptuous hosts.

—Martial (c. A.D. 40–104)
Epigrams

Three-Bean Soup with Brown Rice

Red, white, and green beans in a tomato broth

8 servings

A warming, hearty, high-fiber soup, this is great served with Green Chili Cornbread (page 145) and a simple salad or coleslaw.

2 tablespoons olive oil

1 large onion, chopped

2 to 3 cloves garlic, minced

1 large celery stalk, diced

6 cups water

½ cup raw brown rice, rinsed

One 16-ounce can salt-free crushed tomatoes

1½ teaspoons dried oregano

1 teaspoon chili powder

One 10-ounce package frozen green beans

One 16-ounce can great northern or
   cannellini beans, drained and rinsed

One 16-ounce can kidney or red beans,
   drained and rinsed

1 tablespoon lime juice, or more to taste

¼ cup minced fresh cilantro or parsley

Salt and freshly ground pepper to taste

Thin lime wedges for garnish, optional

Per serving:
Calories: 207   Total fat: 4 g   Protein: 8 g   Fiber: 9 g
Carbohydrate: 35 g   Cholesterol: 0 mg   Sodium: 300 mg

Heat the oil in a soup pot. Add the onion and sauté over medium-low heat until translucent. Add the garlic and celery and continue to sauté until all are golden.

Add the water, rice, tomatoes, oregano, and chili powder. Bring to a rapid simmer, then lower the heat. Cover and simmer gently for 30 minutes.

Add the three types of beans and simmer over very low heat for another 15 to 20 minutes, or until the rice and green beans are quite tender.

Stir in the lime juice and cilantro, then season with salt and pepper. If time allows, let the soup stand off the heat for an hour or longer, then heat through before serving. Garnish each serving with two or three lime wedges, if desired.

Next to the Emperor, rice is the most sacred of all things on earth.

—Japanese proverb

Taco Soup

The zesty flavors of tacos turned inside out

6 servings

The presentation of this easy, offbeat soup is fun and dramatic.

4 cups water

½ cup raw bulgur

1 tablespoon olive oil

1 large onion, chopped

2 to 3 cloves garlic, minced

1 medium green bell pepper, finely diced

4 cups cooked pinto beans (about 1½ cups dried), or two 16-ounce cans, drained and rinsed

One 28-ounce can salt-free crushed tomatoes

¼ cup chopped mild green chilies, fresh or canned, optional

¼ cup chopped fresh cilantro, optional

1 to 2 teaspoons chili powder, or to taste

1 teaspoon ground cumin

1 teaspoon dried oregano

Garnishes:

1 to 1½ cups grated cheddar-style nondairy cheese (see Note)

Thinly shredded romaine or green leaf lettuce

Finely diced firm, ripe tomatoes (about 1 cup)

Large, triangular stone-ground tortilla chips

Per serving:

Calories: 405   Total fat: 12 g   Protein: 16 g   Fiber: 20 g
Carbohydrate: 64 g   Cholesterol: 0 mg   Sodium: 228 mg

Bring 1 cup of the water to a boil in a small saucepan. Add the bulgur and simmer, covered, for 15 minutes, or until the water is absorbed. Or if you can do this step ahead of time, simply add the bulgur to the boiling water, cover, and remove from the heat. Let stand for 30 minutes.

Heat the oil in a soup pot. Add the onion and sauté over medium heat until translucent. Add the garlic and bell pepper and continue to sauté, stirring frequently, until all are golden.

Add the remaining ingredients, except the garnishes, plus the cooked bulgur and the remaining 3 cups water. Bring to a rapid simmer, then lower the heat. Cover and simmer gently for 10 to 15 minutes, then remove from the heat.

Assemble each serving as follows: Fill each bowl about ⅔ full with soup. Top with some grated cheese, shredded lettuce, and diced tomatoes. Line the perimeter of each bowl with several tortilla chips, points facing upward, for a kind of star-shaped effect. The tortilla chips can be used to scoop up the solid parts of the soup or just nibbled along with the soup. Pass around a bowl of extra tortilla chips.

NOTE:

Vegan Gourmet nacho cheese is particularly good in this recipe.

Hearty Barley-Bean Soup

A main-dish soup featuring nourishing grains and beans

6 to 8 servings

This is a good, basic, everyday sort of soup, suitable for cold weather. Try Cheese and Herb Corn Muffins (page 150) as an accompaniment.

2 tablespoons olive oil

2 large onions, chopped

2 to 3 cloves garlic, minced

6 cups water

¾ cup raw pearl or pot barley, rinsed

2 large celery stalks, diced

2 medium carrots, peeled and sliced

Handful of celery leaves

1 bay leaf

2½ teaspoons salt-free seasoning (see
    page 4 for brands)

One 16-ounce can salt-free diced tomatoes,
    undrained

One 16-ounce can kidney, red, or pink beans,
    drained and rinsed

¼ cup chopped fresh parsley

2 tablespoons minced fresh dill

Salt and freshly ground pepper to taste

Per serving:
Calories: 194   Total fat: 4 g   Protein: 8 g   Fiber: 10 g
Carbohydrate: 34 g   Cholesterol: 0 mg   Sodium: 180 mg

Heat the oil in a soup pot. Add the onions and sauté over medium-low heat until translucent. Add the garlic and continue to sauté until both are golden.

Add all the remaining ingredients except the last four. Bring to a rapid simmer, then lower the heat. Cover and simmer gently for 45 to 60 minutes, or until the barley and vegetables are tender.

Add the beans, parsley, and dill. Season with salt and pepper, then simmer for another 15 minutes over low heat. Discard the bay leaf.

Serve at once, or if time allows, let the soup stand off the heat for an hour or so, then heat through before serving. As the soup stands, it will thicken; add water as needed, then adjust the seasonings.

Barley ... is more cooling than wheat, and a little cleansing; and all the preparations thereof do give great nourishment to persons troubled with fevers, agues, and heats in the stomach.

—Nicolas Culpeper (1616–1654)
  Culpeper's Complete Herbal

Tomato, Lentil, and Barley Soup

Another high-protein, warming main-dish soup

6 to 8 servings

Lentil soups are so satisfying in winter. Served with Quick Sunflower-Cheese Bread (page 144) or Focaccia Bread (page 148), this soup needs only a simple salad to make a very filling meal.

1 tablespoon olive oil

1 large onion, chopped

2 to 3 cloves garlic, minced

6 cups water

½ pound raw brown or green lentils, rinsed

¾ cup raw pearl or pot barley, rinsed

2 large celery stalks, diced

2 medium carrots, peeled and sliced

1 cup shredded green cabbage

One 28-ounce can salt-free diced
    tomatoes, undrained

¼ cup dry red wine, optional

1 to 2 tablespoons apple cider vinegar,
    to taste

¼ cup chopped fresh parsley

2 teaspoons salt-free seasoning (see page 4
    for brands)

2 teaspoons paprika

Salt and freshly ground pepper to taste

Per serving:
Calories: 250   Total fat: 3 g   Protein: 13 g   Fiber: 16 g
Carbohydrate: 46 g   Cholesterol: 0 mg   Sodium: 45 mg

Heat the oil in a soup pot. Add the onion and sauté over medium-low heat until translucent. Add the garlic and continue to sauté until both are golden.

Add all the remaining ingredients except the salt and pepper. Bring to a rapid simmer, then lower the heat. Cover and simmer gently for about 45 to 55 minutes, or until the lentils, barley, and vegetables are tender. Stir occasionally and add more water if the soup becomes too thick.

Season with salt and pepper. If time allows, let the soup stand off the heat for an hour or so, then heat through before serving. This soup thickens as it stands; add water as needed and adjust the seasonings.

The philosophers Virgil and Pliny credited lentils with the ability to produce temperaments of mildness and moderation in those who consumed them.

Curried Lentil, Potato, and Cauliflower Soup
with spinach and lots of garlic

6 to 8 servings

This soup features a slew of compatible ingredients made even more companionable in a mildly curried broth.

1½ tablespoons olive oil

1 large onion, chopped

4 to 6 cloves garlic, minced

1 cup raw brown or green lentils, rinsed

1 large celery stalk, diced

6 cups water

2 large potatoes, scrubbed and diced

One 16-ounce can salt-free diced tomatoes, undrained

2 teaspoons good-quality curry powder, or to taste

½ teaspoon turmeric

Pinch of ground nutmeg

2½ cups finely chopped cauliflower pieces

2 cups finely chopped fresh spinach leaves

2 tablespoons minced fresh cilantro

Juice of ½ lemon

Salt and freshly ground pepper to taste

Per serving:
Calories: 219   Total fat: 4 g   Protein: 12 g   Fiber: 13 g
Carbohydrate: 39 g   Cholesterol: 0 mg   Sodium: 49 mg

Heat the oil in a soup pot. Add the onion and sauté over medium-low heat until translucent. Add the garlic and continue to sauté until both are golden.

Add the lentils, celery, and water. Bring to a rapid simmer, then lower the heat. Cover and simmer gently for 10 minutes.

Add the potatoes, tomatoes, curry powder, turmeric, and nutmeg, and simmer until the potatoes are about half done, about 10 to 15 minutes. Add the cauliflower and simmer until the lentils and vegetables are tender, about 20 minutes longer.

Stir in the spinach, cilantro, and lemon juice. Adjust the consistency with more water as needed, then season with salt and pepper. Simmer over very low heat for another 5 minutes. Serve at once, or if time allows, let stand off the heat for an hour or so, then heat through before serving.

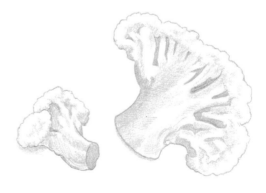

Four-Grain Tomato Soup

A sublime medley of whole grains and vegetables in a tomato base

8 or more servings

For a hearty combination, serve with Hearty Bean Bread (page 146), or for a lighter accompaniment, serve with Bruschetta (page 159).

2 tablespoons olive oil

2 medium onions, quartered and thinly sliced

2 large celery stalks, finely diced

2 medium carrots, peeled and finely diced

2 medium potatoes, scrubbed and diced,
    or 2 large turnips, peeled and diced

One 28-ounce can salt-free pureed or
    crushed tomatoes

¼ cup raw brown rice, any variety, rinsed
    (see Note)

¼ cup raw wild rice, rinsed

¼ cup raw millet or quinoa, rinsed

¼ cup raw pearl barley, rinsed

2 bay leaves

2 teaspoons salt-free seasoning (see page 4
    for brands)

6 cups water

¼ cup chopped fresh dill

Salt and freshly ground pepper to taste

Per serving:
Calories: 193   Total fat: 4 g   Protein: 6 g   Fiber: 6 g
Carbohydrate: 37 g   Cholesterol: 0 mg   Sodium: 55 mg

Heat the oil in a soup pot. Add the onions and sauté over medium-low heat for 5 to 8 minutes, until translucent.

Add all the remaining ingredients except the dill, salt, and pepper. Bring to a rapid simmer, then lower the heat. Cover and simmer gently for 1 hour, stirring every 15 minutes or so.

If the soup is too thick, adjust the consistency with more water as needed, and return to a gentle simmer. Stir in the dill and season with salt and pepper. Simmer gently for 15 to 20 minutes longer, or until the grains and vegetables are completely tender. Discard the bay leaves.

Serve at once, or if time allows, let the soup stand off the heat for an hour or two, then heat through before serving. This soup thickens quite a bit as it stands. Add water and adjust the seasonings as needed.

NOTE:
If you use brown basmati rice, the soup will be wonderfully aromatic as it is cooked and served.

Potage Polenta

Cornmeal porridge enlivened with fresh and dried tomatoes and red beans

6 to 8 servings

Cooked cornmeal makes a delightfully dense soup base. Serve this meal-in-a-bowl with a bountiful salad and crusty bread.

2 tablespoons olive oil

3 to 4 cloves garlic, minced

6 cups water

1 cup yellow cornmeal, preferably stone-
  ground

One 16-ounce can small red beans, drained
  and rinsed

1 medium-small zucchini, quartered
  lengthwise and sliced

1 cup diced ripe tomatoes

¼ cup oil-cured sun-dried tomatoes, plus
  more for topping if desired

1 teaspoon Italian herb seasoning

6 to 8 ounces Swiss chard or spinach, well
  washed, stemmed, and chopped

Salt and freshly ground pepper to taste

Handful of basil leaves, cut into strips

½ cup grated mozzarella-style nondairy
  cheese for topping, optional

Per serving:
Calories: 184   Total fat: 6 g   Protein: 6 g   Fiber: 7 g
Carbohydrate: 29 g   Cholesterol: 0 mg   Sodium: 235 mg

Heat the oil in a soup pot. Add the garlic and sauté over low heat until golden.

Add 4 cups of the water and bring to a gentle simmer. Pour the cornmeal into the pot in a thin, steady stream, ¼ cup at a time, whisking constantly.

Stir in the beans, zucchini, tomatoes, dried tomatoes, and seasoning. Cover and continue to simmer gently. Uncover to whisk well every 5 minutes or so, for 25 minutes, or until the cornmeal is cooked. Whisk in 1 cup of water with each of the last two stirrings.

Stir in the chard or spinach. Cook for an additional 7 to 10 minutes for the chard and 3 to 5 minutes for the spinach, just until tender but still bright green. Adjust the consistency with more water if needed. The soup should be fairly thick, but thinner than a cornmeal porridge.

Season with salt and pepper and serve. Top each serving with a a few strips of basil, and if desired, a sprinkling of cheese and a few extra strips of dried tomato.

The word soupe is French, but extremely bourgeois; it is well to serve potage and not soupe.

—*Dictionnaire de Trévoux* (18th century)

Vegetarian Goulash

The Hungarian "meat and potatoes" stew made with seitan

8 servings

A satisfying meatless take on the classic Hungarian goulash, this makes good use of seitan, a high-protein, low-fat meat substitute.

2 ½ tablespoons olive oil

1½ cups chopped onion

2 cloves garlic, minced

2 tablespoons unbleached white flour

4 medium potatoes, scrubbed and cut into
    ¾-inch chunks

3 medium carrots, peeled and sliced

One 16-ounce can salt-free diced tomatoes,
    undrained

¼ cup dry red wine, optional

1 tablespoon paprika

4 cups water with 2 vegetable bouillon cubes,
    or other stock option (page 9)

2 cups frozen green beans, thawed

½ cup minced fresh parsley

1 tablespoon reduced-sodium soy sauce

1 pound seitan, cut into bite-sized chunks

Salt and freshly ground pepper to taste

Per serving:
Calories: 224   Total fat: 6 g   Protein: 19 g   Fiber: 5 g
Carbohydrate: 27 g   Cholesterol: 0 mg   Sodium: 400 mg

Heat about half of the oil in a soup pot. Add the onion and sauté over medium-low heat until translucent. Add the garlic and continue to sauté until both are golden.

Sprinkle in the flour, stirring in until well blended with the onion. Add the potatoes, carrots, tomatoes, optional wine, paprika, and water with bouillon cubes. Bring to a rapid simmer, then lower the heat. Cover and simmer gently for 30 minutes.

Add the green beans and half of the parsley, then simmer gently for 15 minutes longer.

Meanwhile, slowly heat the remaining oil together with the soy sauce in a skillet. Add the seitan chunks and stir quickly to coat with the oil and soy sauce mixture. Raise the heat to medium-high and sauté, stirring frequently, until the chunks are somewhat crisp and golden on most sides. Remove from the heat and stir into the stew.

Adjust the consistency with water if too dense, but let the soup remain thick rather than soupy. Season with salt and pepper. Serve at once, or if time allows, let stand for an hour or two, then heat through before serving. Top each serving with a sprinkling of the remaining parsley.

Thai-Spiced Sweet Potato Stew

Nourishing sweet potatoes in a delectable coconut base

6 servings

With Thai ingredients available at most natural food stores and well-stocked supermarkets, it has become easy to enjoy the delightful flavors of this cuisine at home. Use your discretion with the red or green curry paste; a little will give a hint of heat, but if you want a spicier stew, you can step it up from there.

1 tablespoon olive oil

1 medium onion, quartered and thinly sliced

4 to 6 cloves garlic, minced

3 medium-large sweet potatoes (about 1½ pounds), peeled and diced

3 cups water

1 medium green or red bell pepper, cut into short, narrow strips

1½ cups frozen green beans

½ teaspoon red or green curry paste, more or less to taste

1 tablespoon natural granulated sugar

2 teaspoons minced fresh ginger

2 stalks lemongrass, optional

One 13.5-ounce can light coconut milk

2 tablespoons smooth or chunky natural peanut butter

Salt to taste

One 8-ounce package White Wave Thai peanut-flavored baked tofu, diced, optional

Cilantro leaves for topping

Per serving:
Calories: 290   Total fat: 10 g   Protein: 14 g   Fiber: 6 g
Carbohydrate: 42 g   Cholesterol: 0 mg   Sodium: 235 mg

Heat the oil in a soup pot. Add the onion and sauté over medium-low heat until translucent. Add the garlic and continue to sauté until both are golden.

Add the sweet potatoes and water. Bring to a rapid simmer, then lower the heat. Cover and simmer for 10 minutes, or until the sweet potatoes are about half done.

Add the bell pepper, green beans, curry paste, sugar, and ginger. If using lemongrass, cut each stalk into 3 or 4 pieces, and bruise by making long cuts here and there with a sharp knife. This will help release the lemony flavor. Stir into the soup pot. Simmer the stew for 10 minutes longer.

Stir in the coconut milk, peanut butter, salt, and optional tofu. Return to a simmer, then cook over very low heat for another 10 minutes, or until all the vegetables are tender and the flavors well integrated.

Remove the lemongrass pieces. Taste to adjust seasonings, particularly the curry paste if you'd like a spicier stew, as well as the salt, sugar, and ginger. Serve at once, topping each serving with a few cilantro leaves.

Miso Soup with Winter Vegetables

Surprisingly substantial, with roots, cabbage, and tofu

6 servings

This soup is very warming, and more filling than more common, very brothy miso soups.

1 tablespoon olive oil

2 medium onions, quartered and sliced

4 medium potatoes, peeled and finely diced (see Variation)

1½ cups shredded green cabbage, preferably napa

1 large celery stalk, cut into thick matchsticks

1 large carrot, peeled and cut into thick matchsticks

1 cup peeled, diced daikon radish, turnip, or parsnip

1 recipe Asian Mushroom Broth (page 15), shiitake mushrooms reserved

8 ounces soft tofu, blotted and cut into small dice

¼ cup dry red wine or sherry

1 teaspoon grated fresh ginger

2 to 3 tablespoons miso, any variety, to taste

Freshly ground pepper to taste

Per serving:
Calories: 199   Total fat: 6 g   Protein: 7 g   Fiber: 4 g
Carbohydrate: 30 g   Cholesterol: 0 mg   Sodium: 565 mg

Heat the oil in a soup pot. Add the onions and sauté over medium-low heat until golden.

Add the potatoes, cabbage, celery, carrot, and daikon radish. Cover with the broth.

Trim the shiitake mushrooms used in making the broth of their tough stems, then slice the caps and add them to the soup along with the tofu, wine, and ginger. Bring to a rapid simmer, then lower the heat. Cover and simmer gently for 20 to 25 minutes, or until the vegetables are done. Remove from the heat.

Dissolve the miso in just enough water to make it smooth and pourable. Stir it into the soup, then taste to see if you'd like to add more. Season with plenty of pepper and serve at once.

VARIATION:
Substitute one medium sweet potato for two of the white potatoes.

Vietnamese "Beef" Noodle Soup

The classic *Pho Bo* made faux with seitan

6 servings

This Asian soup is brimming with invigorating flavors and textures. I love it as a change of pace in the winter from thick soups and stews. It's still every bit as warming. Despite the length of the ingredient list, this is a quick soup—you'll be eating in about half an hour.

3- to 4-ounce bundle fine rice noodles or
   bean-thread noodles
1 tablespoon olive oil
3 to 4 cloves garlic, minced
1 shallot, minced
One 32-ounce carton low-sodium
   vegetable broth
One 5- to 6-inch piece kombu
   (sea vegetable), optional
2 tablespoons reduced-sodium soy sauce, or
   more to taste
1 teaspoon minced fresh ginger, or more
   to taste
½ teaspoon five-spice powder
2 cups water
6 to 8 ounces seitan, cut into thin shreds
1 cup fresh mung bean sprouts
4 scallions, thinly sliced
¼ cup minced fresh cilantro
2 teaspoons lime juice, or more to taste
Freshly ground pepper to taste
Thinly sliced lime sections for garnish

Per serving:
Calories: 132   Total fat: 3 g   Protein: 10 g   Fiber: 1 g
Carbohydrate: 17 g   Cholesterol: 0 mg   Sodium: 560 mg

Cook the noodles according to package directions until *al dente*, then drain and cut into shorter lengths suitable for soup. Set aside until needed.

Meanwhile, heat the oil in a soup pot. Add the garlic and shallot and sauté over medium-low heat until both are golden.

Add the broth, optional kombu, soy sauce, ginger, five-spice powder, and water. Bring to a rapid simmer, then lower the heat. Cover and simmer gently for 10 minutes.

Add the seitan, bean sprouts, half of the scallions, and half of the cilantro. Season with lime juice, pepper, and if desired, some additional soy sauce. Simmer for 3 minutes longer, then remove from the heat.

Serve at once, garnishing the top of each serving with a thin slice or two of lime, and the remaining cilantro and scallions.

SPRING

After the thick, hearty soups of winter, those presented here offer the palate a lift with lighter textures and flavors. These soups set the stage for a meal, taking the edge off of hunger yet leaving room for other courses.

Spring Vegetable Soup

Potatoes, carrots, mushrooms, and peas in a light dilled broth

8 or more servings

Brimming with fresh produce in a light, mildly seasoned broth, this is just the soup to serve as an introduction to a festive spring meal such as Easter dinner or the Passover seder.

2 tablespoons olive oil

1 medium onion, finely chopped

2 large or 3 medium leeks, white parts
   only, quartered lengthwise, chopped,
   and well rinsed

6 cups water with 2 vegetable bouillon cubes,
   or other stock option (page 9)

2 medium potatoes, peeled and diced

3 medium carrots, peeled and sliced

3 medium celery stalks, diced

8 ounces white, baby bella, or crimini
   mushrooms, sliced

1 teaspoon paprika

1 teaspoon ground cumin

Salt and freshly ground pepper to taste

¼ cup minced fresh dill, or more to taste

2 cups frozen green peas, thawed

Per serving:
Calories: 136   Total fat: 4 g   Protein: 5 g   Fiber: 5 g
Carbohydrate: 21 g   Cholesterol: 0 mg   Sodium: 111 mg

Heat the oil in a soup pot. Add the onion and leeks and sauté over medium heat until the leeks are limp, about 10 minutes.

Add the water with bouillon cubes, potatoes, carrots, celery, mushrooms, paprika, and cumin. Bring to a rapid simmer, then lower the heat. Cover and simmer gently for about 30 minutes, or until the vegetables are tender.

Season with salt and pepper. Let stand for an hour or two to develop flavor. Just before serving, add the dill and peas and reheat.

Greek-Flavored Spinach and Orzo Soup

Leeks, greens, and tiny pasta in a lemony broth

6 to 8 servings

Here's a lively soup that comes together quickly. Serve with a big Greek-style salad and a fresh flatbread for a light yet satisfying meal.

1½ tablespoons olive oil

1 cup chopped, well-washed leek, white part only

1 large red bell pepper, diced

2 to 3 cloves garlic, minced

6 cups water with 2 vegetable bouillon cubes, or other stock option (page 9)

One 16-ounce can salt-free Italian-style stewed tomatoes, undrained

¾ cup orzo (rice-shaped pasta)

5 to 6 ounces fresh spinach (regular or baby spinach), well washed, stemmed, and chopped

¼ cup chopped fresh parsley or dill, or a combination, or more to taste

Juice of 1 lemon

Salt and freshly ground pepper to taste

Per serving:

Calories: 136   Total fat: 4 g   Protein: 4 g   Fiber: 2 g
Carbohydrate: 21 g   Cholesterol: 0 mg   Sodium: 203 mg

Heat the oil in a soup pot. Add the leek and sauté over medium heat until translucent, about 5 minutes. Add the red pepper and garlic and sauté the vegetables for another 5 to 8 minutes, or until the leek turns golden and the pepper softens.

Add the water with bouillon cubes. Drain the liquid from the canned tomatoes into the soup pot, then chop the tomatoes finely before adding to the soup. Bring to a rapid simmer, then lower the heat. Cover and simmer gently for 10 minutes.

Meanwhile, cook the orzo in a separate saucepan until *al dente*, then drain. Add the cooked orzo to the soup along with the spinach and herbs.

Stir in the lemon juice. If the soup is too dense, add a small amount of water. Season with salt and pepper. Simmer over very low heat until well heated through, then serve.

When buying spinach, assess its liveliness. It should have a bouncing, bright appearance. As you stuff it into your basket ... it should crunch and squeak.

—Jane Grigson
  Jane Grigson's Vegetable Book, 1978

Potage Maigre

A traditional Creole soup featuring lettuce, cucumber, and peas

6 to 8 servings

This light soup of lettuce, cucumber, and fresh spring peas was quite common in nineteenth-century America. Potage maigre translates loosely as "fast day" soup, traditionally made for Lent. Versions of it appear in old Creole cookbooks.

2 tablespoons olive oil

2 large onions, quartered and thinly sliced

1 large celery stalk, finely diced

Handful of celery leaves

2 small heads Boston or Bibb lettuce, finely shredded

One 32-ounce carton low-sodium vegetable broth

1 cup water

1 cup steamed fresh or thawed frozen green peas

1 cup peeled, seeded, and finely diced cucumber

¼ cup chopped fresh parsley

2 tablespoons chopped fresh dill

Salt and freshly ground pepper to taste

Vegan Sour Cream (page 7) for topping, optional

Per serving:
Calories: 85   Total fat: 5 g   Protein: 3 g   Fiber: 3 g
Carbohydrate: 9 g   Cholesterol: 0 mg   Sodium: 77 mg

Heat the oil in a soup pot. Add the onions and sauté over medium-low heat until translucent. Add the celery and continue to sauté until the onions are golden.

Add the celery leaves, lettuce, broth, and water. Bring to a rapid simmer, then lower the heat.

Add the peas and cucumber. Adjust the consistency with additional water if the soup is too dense. Stir in the parsley and dill, then season with salt and lots of freshly ground pepper. Simmer over very low heat for 5 minutes.

Serve at once, or allow to cool to room temperature to serve. Either way, top each serving with a dollop of sour cream, if desired.

Young green peas! Do not these words sound pleasant to the ear ... I fancy that, by merely raising my eyes from the paper on which I am now writing, I shall see all our garden in bud and blossom.

—Alexia Soyer
The Modern Housewife, 1851

Asparagus and Spinach Soup
with wild rice and mushrooms

6 servings

You'll love making and serving this earthy medley of colors, textures, and flavors on a rainy spring evening.

1¼ cups water

½ cup raw wild rice, rinsed

10 to 12 ounces asparagus

4 to 6 ounces fresh wild mushrooms, such as shiitake or porcini, or a combination of 2 or 3 kinds

1 large carrot, peeled and coarsely grated

1 medium yellow summer squash, diced

4 to 5 scallions, white and green parts, sliced

One 32-ounce carton low-sodium vegetable broth

1½ teaspoons salt-free seasoning (see page 4 for brands)

¼ cup dry white wine, optional

5 to 6 ounces fresh spinach, well washed, stemmed, and chopped

Salt and freshly ground pepper to taste

Per serving:
Calories: 94   Total fat: 1 g   Protein: 5 g   Fiber: 4 g
Carbohydrate: 19 g   Cholesterol: 0 mg   Sodium: 273 mg

Bring the water to a boil in a small saucepan. Add the wild rice, then cover and simmer gently until the water is absorbed, about 35 minutes.

Meanwhile, trim the asparagus of its woody ends and peel the bottom halves of the stalks with a vegetable peeler. Cut into 1-inch pieces.

Combine the asparagus with the remaining ingredients, except the last two, in a soup pot. There should be enough liquid to just cover the vegetables; add water as needed. Bring to a rapid simmer, then lower the heat. Cover and simmer gently for about 15 minutes, or until the vegetables are just tender. Remove from the heat.

When the wild rice is done, stir it into the soup, followed by the spinach. Cover and cook until the spinach has wilted, then season with salt and pepper. Adjust the consistency with more water if needed, to give the soup a slightly dense consistency.

If time allows, let the soup stand off the heat for an hour or two to develop flavor. Heat through before serving.

Asparagus is a delicate fruit, and wholesome for everiebodie, and especially when it is thicke, tender and sweet ... it maketh a good color in the face.

—Anonymous
  Maison Rustique, 1600

Puree of Asparagus with Soba Noodles
and a garnish of toasted almonds

6 servings

Nutty-tasting Japanese soba (buckwheat noodles) add an offbeat touch to this soup. Look for them in natural food stores or Asian groceries.

2 pounds asparagus

1 tablespoon dark sesame oil

1 large onion, chopped

One 32-ounce carton low-sodium
  vegetable broth

2 large celery stalks, diced

2 medium potatoes, scrubbed and diced

2 teaspoons salt-free seasoning
  (see page 4 for brands)

2 tablespoons reduced-sodium soy sauce, or
  more to taste

4 ounces soba, any variety

Freshly ground pepper to taste

½ cup slivered or sliced almonds, toasted,
  for garnish

Sliced scallions or minced chives for garnish

Per serving:
Calories: 226   Total fat: 7 g   Protein: 10 g   Fiber: 6 g
Carbohydrate: 37 g   Cholesterol: 0 mg   Sodium: 586 mg

Trim the woody ends from the asparagus, peel the bottom halves with a vegetable peeler, and cut into 1-inch lengths. Reserve and set aside the tips.

Heat the oil in a large soup pot. Add the onion and sauté over medium heat until golden. Add the broth, celery, potatoes, seasoning, and soy sauce. Bring to a rapid simmer, then lower the heat. Cover and simmer gently for 10 minutes.

Add the asparagus pieces (except for the reserved tips) and simmer for another 15 minutes, or until the vegetables are tender. Remove from the heat.

With a slotted spoon, transfer the solid ingredients to a food processor. Puree in batches until smooth and stir back into the liquid in the soup pot. Or insert an immersion blender into the soup pot and puree until smooth. Let the soup stand off the heat while doing the finishing steps.

Break the buckwheat noodles into 1- to- 2-inch lengths. In a separate saucepan, cook them in rapidly simmering water until *al dente*. Drain and rinse them briefly under cool water, then stir into the soup.

In the same saucepan, steam the reserved asparagus tips until bright green and tender-crisp, then stir into the soup.

Adjust the consistency of the soup with enough water to give it a slightly thick consistency. Season with freshly ground pepper and additional soy sauce, if needed. Serve at once, garnishing each serving with the almonds and scallions.

Spicy Asparagus and Green Bean Stew
with red peppers and baked tofu

6 servings

I recommend steaming the green beans separately, and adding them once the asparagus is tender-crisp. The result is a satisfying Asian-flavored stew with the green vegetables all done just right.

1 pound fresh green beans, trimmed and
    cut in half

1 tablespoon dark sesame oil

1 medium onion, finely chopped

4 to 5 cloves garlic, minced

2 cups water

1 pound slender asparagus, woody ends
    trimmed, cut into 1½-inch lengths

2 medium red bell peppers, cut into narrow
    strips approximately 1½ inches in length

2 to 3 teaspoons grated fresh ginger, to taste

¼ cup dry red wine, optional

One 8-ounce package Thai- or teriyaki-
    flavored baked tofu, diced

1 teaspoon Thai chili paste, or to taste

1 tablespoon rice vinegar or
    white wine vinegar

2 to 3 tablespoons reduced-sodium soy
    sauce, to taste

2 tablespoons cornstarch

Hot cooked rice or noodles, optional

Per serving:
Calories: 169   Total fat: 7 g   Protein: 11 g   Fiber: 5 g
Carbohydrate: 19 g   Cholesterol: 0 mg   Sodium: 355 mg

In a large saucepan, steam the green beans in an inch or so of water, covered, until tender-crisp. Stir occasionally. When done, remove from the heat and rinse briefly with cool water.

In the meantime, heat the oil in a soup pot or large steep-sided wok. Add the onion and garlic and sauté over medium heat, stirring frequently, until the onion is lightly golden. Add the water, asparagus, red pepper strips, ginger, and optional wine. Bring to a simmer, then lower the heat. Cover and simmer gently for 10 minutes, or until the asparagus and red pepper strips are tender-crisp.

Add the tofu, chili paste, vinegar, and soy sauce. Once the green beans are done, add them as well. Stir gently and bring the mixture to a simmer.

Dissolve the cornstarch in a small amount of water. Pour slowly into the stew, stirring. Simmer over low heat, uncovered, for 5 minutes longer. Serve at once on its own or over hot cooked rice or noodles.

Parsley-Potato Soup
with a luscious cream cheese base

6 to 8 servings

Lots of fresh parsley and a touch of cream cheese give this soup its special character. Serve with crusty French or Italian bread.

1 tablespoon olive oil

1 large onion, chopped

2 cloves garlic, minced

4 cups water with 2 vegetable bouillon cubes, or other stock option (page 9)

6 medium potatoes, preferably a mealy variety like russet, peeled and diced

2 bay leaves

4 ounces vegan cream cheese, diced

½ cup firmly packed chopped fresh parsley

2 tablespoons minced fresh dill

¼ cup quick-cooking oats

2 cups rice milk, or as needed

Salt and freshly ground pepper to taste

Per serving:
Calories: 193   Total fat: 5 g   Protein: 6 g   Fiber: 3 g
Carbohydrate: 32 g   Cholesterol: 0 mg   Sodium: 84 mg

Heat the oil in a soup pot. Add the onion and sauté over medium-low heat until translucent. Add the garlic and continue to sauté until both are golden.

Add the water with bouillon cubes, potatoes, and bay leaves. Bring to a rapid simmer, then lower the heat. Cover and simmer gently until the potatoes are just tender, about 20 to 25 minutes.

Remove about ½ cup of the hot liquid with a ladle and transfer it to a small mixing bowl. Combine with the cream cheese and whisk together until smooth and creamy. Stir into the soup along with the parsley and dill.

Slowly sprinkle in the oats. Simmer for another 20 to 25 minutes over very low heat, or until the potatoes are completely tender.

Add enough rice milk to give the soup a slightly thick consistency, then season with salt and pepper. Discard the bay leaves. Heat through and serve. This soup thickens as it stands; thin as needed with additional rice milk, then adjust the seasonings.

Never cut parsley if you are in love. If you give it away, you also give away your luck.

—Old European folk belief

Leek and Mushroom Bisque

A simple spring soup with a Cream of Wheat backdrop

6 to 8 servings

Cream of Wheat, or farina, is the secret to the smooth, thick texture of this soup.

3 large leeks, white and palest green
  parts only
2 tablespoons olive oil
4 cups water with 2 vegetable bouillon
  cubes, or other stock option (page 9)
One 16-ounce can salt-free pureed tomatoes
½ cup Cream of Wheat
12 ounces mushrooms, coarsely chopped
  or sliced
2 teaspoons salt-free seasoning (see
  page 4 for brands)
1½ to 2 cups rice milk, or as needed
Salt and freshly ground pepper to taste

Per serving:
Calories: 178   Total fat: 5 g   Protein: 5 g   Fiber: 3 g
Carbohydrate: 30 g   Cholesterol: 0 mg   Sodium: 96 mg

As long as you have eaten the strong-smelling shoots of Tarentine leeks, give kisses with shut mouth.

—Martial (c. A.D. 40–104)
  Epigrams

Cut the white and pale green parts of the leeks in half lengthwise, then into ¼-inch slices. Rinse well to remove
all grit.

Heat the oil in a soup pot. Add the leeks and sauté over medium heat until limp. Add the water with bouillon cubes and the pureed tomatoes. Bring to a rapid simmer, then lower the heat until the liquid is at a very gentle simmer. Slowly sprinkle in the farina, whisking it in as you do.

Add the mushrooms and the seasoning. Cover and simmer gently for 20 minutes.

Stir in enough rice milk to give the soup a slightly thick consistency, then season with salt and pepper. Simmer for another 5 minutes.

Remove from the heat and let the soup stand off the heat for at least an hour. Heat through, then adjust the consistency with more rice milk if necessary before serving. Adjust the seasonings, then serve.

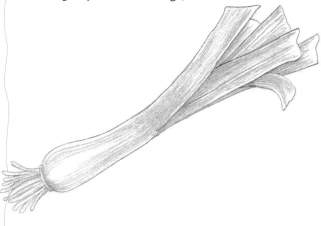

Puree of Broccoli Soup with Whole Wheat Pasta

A glorious green soup with a dried-tomato garnish

6 or more servings

If you like broccoli, you'll love this nourishing bowl of comfort.

2 stalks broccoli with large crowns

2 tablespoons extra-virgin olive oil

2 medium onions, chopped

2 cloves garlic, minced

1 large celery stalk, diced

2 tablespoons unbleached white flour

1 large tomato, chopped

¼ cup firmly packed chopped fresh parsley

2 teaspoons salt-free seasoning
   (see page 4 for brands)

2 cups rice milk, or as needed

1 cup small whole wheat shell or elbow pasta

Salt and freshly ground pepper to taste

6 to 8 oil-cured sun-dried tomatoes, cut into
   strips for garnish

Per serving:
Calories: 158   Total fat: 6 g   Protein: 3 g   Fiber: 3 g
Carbohydrate: 24 g   Cholesterol: 0 mg   Sodium: 56 mg

Finely chop the broccoli, then set aside about 1½ cups of the florets.

Heat the oil in a large soup pot. Add the onions, garlic, and celery and sauté over medium-low heat until the onions are golden. Slowly sprinkle in the flour, stirring it in until it disappears.

Add the chopped broccoli (except for the reserved florets), tomato, parsley, seasoning, and enough water to cover all but about ½ inch of the vegetables. Bring to a rapid simmer, then lower the heat. Cover and simmer gently for 15 to 20 minutes, or until the broccoli is tender but not overdone. Remove from the heat.

Transfer the solid ingredients with a slotted spoon to a food processor or blender and puree, in batches if necessary, until smooth. Stir back into the soup pot and add enough rice milk to give the soup a slightly thick consistency. Or insert an immersion blender into the pot and process until pureed. Let the soup stand off the heat while completing the last steps.

Cook the pasta in a separate saucepan in rapidly simmering water until *al dente*. Drain and rinse briefly under cool water, then stir into the soup. In the same saucepan, steam the reserved broccoli florets until bright green and tender-crisp. Stir into the soup.

Return the soup to medium-low heat. Adjust the consistency of the soup with more rice milk as needed, then season to taste with salt and pepper. Let the soup remain on very low heat for another 5 minutes, then serve. Garnish each serving with a few sun-dried tomato strips.

Curried Red Lentil Soup, page 27

"Buddha's Delight" Stew, page 46

Mock Chicken Noodle Soup, page 54

Taco Soup, page 70

Puree of Spring Greens, page 91

Southeast Asian–Style Vegetable Stew, page 105

Tomato-Mango Coconut Cooler, page 123

Muffins (from background to foreground):
Cheese and Herb Corn Muffins, page 150; Oat-Walnut Muffins, page 151;
Currant Griddle Scones, page 156; and Whole Wheat Vegetable Muffins, page 149

Puree of Spring Greens

An intense blend of Asian greens, spinach, lettuce, and parsley

6 to 8 servings

For some years, my family has belonged to a community-supported farm. In late spring, there is a plethora of greens of all kinds—Asian greens, spinach, and lettuce. At some point there seems to be more than can be used in a week, even by my veggie-loving family. That's when I turn to this recipe—it has become an annual tradition! Make sure all greens are very well washed.

2 tablespoons olive oil

1 large onion, chopped

2 to 3 cloves garlic, minced

3 cups water with 2 vegetable bouillon cubes, or other stock option (page 9)

2 large potatoes, peeled and diced

1 bunch Asian greens, any variety, thick midribs trimmed, leaves coarsely chopped (see Note)

8 to 10 ounces fresh spinach, well washed and stemmed

2 heads green lettuce, coarsely chopped

½ to 1 cup parsley leaves

1 to 2 cups rice milk, or as needed

Salt and freshly ground pepper to taste

Silk creamer for garnish, optional

Per serving:
Calories: 128   Total fat: 5 g   Protein: 4 g   Fiber: 3 g
Carbohydrate: 18 g   Cholesterol: 0 mg   Sodium: 107 mg

Heat the oil in a soup pot. Add the onion and sauté until translucent. Add the garlic and continue to sauté until the onion is golden.

Add the water with bouillon cubes and the potatoes. Bring to a rapid simmer, then lower the heat. Cover and simmer gently until the potatoes are tender, about 15 to 20 minutes.

Add the Asian greens and cover. Simmer gently for 5 minutes. Add the spinach leaves and cover; cook just until they wilt down.

Add the lettuce and parsley and simmer over low heat for 5 minutes, or until all the greens are just tender.

Puree the mixture in batches until smooth in a food processor. Return to the soup pot and stir in enough rice milk to give the soup a slightly thick consistency. Season with salt and pepper and serve.

For an optional, pretty garnish, pour some creamer into a small-spouted pitcher and pour a spiral design onto the top of each serving.

NOTE:

For Asian greens, you can use a small bunch of regular or baby bok choy, tatsoi, or mizuna.

Cream of Cauliflower Soup

A mild puree with a flourish of colorful vegetables

6 servings

This dairy-free "cream" soup, enhanced with any of the garnishes recommended, makes a hearty (but not heavy) introduction for a spring meal.

1 tablespoon olive oil

1 cup chopped onion

2 to 4 cloves garlic, minced

4 cups water with 2 vegetable bouillon cubes, or other stock option (page 9)

1 large head cauliflower, coarsely chopped

2 medium potatoes, peeled and diced

2 teaspoons salt-free seasoning (see page 4 for brands)

1 teaspoon ground cumin

1 cup canned great northern beans or cannellini, drained and rinsed

1½ to 2 cups rice milk, or as needed

¼ cup Silk creamer

Salt and freshly ground pepper to taste

Garnishes (choose any 2 or 3):

Steamed, finely chopped broccoli florets (about 1 cup)

Steamed chopped spinach (about 1 cup)

Steamed fresh green peas (about ¾ cup)

Steamed red bell pepper strips (from 1 medium bell pepper)

Per serving:
Calories: 206   Total fat: 5 g   Protein: 9 g   Fiber: 7 g
Carbohydrate: 35 g   Cholesterol: 0 mg   Sodium: 126 mg

Heat the oil in a soup pot and add the onion. Sauté over medium-low heat until translucent. Add the garlic and continue to sauté until both are golden.

Add the water with bouillon cubes, cauliflower, potatoes, seasoning, and cumin. Bring to a rapid simmer, then lower the heat. Cover and simmer gently for about 20 minutes, or until the vegetables are tender. Remove from the heat.

Transfer the vegetables to a food processor or blender with a slotted spoon and puree, in batches if necessary, until smooth. Puree about half of the beans with each batch of vegetables. Transfer the puree back into the soup pot, stirring it back into whatever liquid remains. Or add all the beans to the soup pot, insert an immersion blender, and process until the soup is smoothly pureed.

Stir in enough rice milk to give the soup a medium-thick consistency, then add the creamer. Season with salt and pepper. If time allows, let the soup stand off the heat for 1 to 2 hours, then heat through before serving. Top each serving with 2 or 3 of the garnishes.

Curried Cauliflower-Cheese Soup

A chunky, mildly spiced soup with the fresh flavors of peas and dill

6 to 8 servings

If you're looking for a mild, soothing soup for a rainy spring evening, here's a pleasant choice.

2 tablespoons olive oil

1 large onion, chopped

2 medium celery stalks, diced

4 cups water with 2 vegetable bouillon cubes, or other stock option (page 9)

3 medium potatoes, peeled and diced

1 medium head cauliflower, finely chopped

2 teaspoons good-quality curry powder, more or less to taste

1½ to 2 cups rice milk, or as needed

¼ cup Silk creamer

1 cup steamed fresh or thawed frozen green peas

2 to 3 tablespoons minced fresh dill or 2 teaspoons dried

1 cup firmly packed grated Monterey Jack or mozzarella-style nondairy cheese

Salt and freshly ground pepper to taste

Per serving:
Calories: 220   Total fat: 11 g   Protein: 6 g   Fiber: 6 g
Carbohydrate: 27 g   Cholesterol: 0 mg   Sodium: 186 mg

Heat the oil in a soup pot. Add the onion and celery and sauté over medium-low heat until both are golden.

Add the water with bouillon cubes, potatoes, cauliflower, and curry powder. Bring to a rapid simmer, then lower the heat. Cover and simmer gently for about 20 to 25 minutes, or until all the vegetables are tender. Remove from the heat.

With a slotted spoon, transfer half of the solid ingredients to a food processor or blender. Process until smoothly pureed. Stir back into the remaining soup. Or insert an immersion blender into the soup and process until about half of the ingredients are pureed.

Add just enough rice milk to give the soup a slightly thick consistency. Stir in the creamer, peas, and dill, then return to low heat and bring to a gentle simmer.

Sprinkle in the cheese a little at a time, stirring until fairly well melted each time. Season to taste with salt and pepper. Simmer gently for 2 to 3 minutes longer, then serve.

Curried Cashew-Vegetable Soup

with notes of ginger, curry, and citrus

6 to 8 servings

Cashew butter makes an offbeat, rich-tasting soup base. This luscious soup is good hot or at room temperature.

1½ tablespoons olive oil

2 large onions, chopped

3 to 4 cloves garlic, minced

1 large celery stalk, diced

4 cups water

1 cup cashew butter

2 teaspoons minced fresh ginger, or to taste

2 teaspoons good-quality curry powder, more
    or less to taste

1 teaspoon ground cumin

Pinch of ground nutmeg

1 tablespoon lemon juice, or more to taste

½ cup orange juice, preferably fresh

3 cups steamed fresh green vegetables (such
    as finely chopped broccoli, green peas,
    diced zucchini, cut green beans,
    or any combination)

Salt and freshly ground pepper to taste

Thinly sliced scallions for garnish

Chopped cashews for garnish, optional

Per serving:
Calories: 228   Total fat: 21 g   Protein: 9 g   Fiber: 4 g
Carbohydrate: 20 g   Cholesterol: 0 mg   Sodium: 29 mg

Heat the oil in a soup pot. Add the onions, garlic, and celery and sauté over medium-low heat until all are lightly browned. Transfer to a food processor with 1 cup of the water and process until smoothly pureed, then transfer back to the soup pot. Or add 1 cup of the water to the soup pot and process with an immersion blender until pureed.

Add the remaining 3 cups water and bring to a rapid simmer. Whisk in the cashew butter, about ⅓ cup at a time.

Stir in the ginger, curry powder, cumin, nutmeg, lemon juice, and orange juice. Return to a rapid simmer, then lower the heat. Cover and simmer gently for 15 minutes.

Stir in the steamed vegetables. If the soup is too thick, add enough water to give the soup a slightly thick consistency. Season with salt and pepper, then serve. Garnish each serving with a sprinkling of scallions and, if desired, a few chopped cashews.

Thick soup served in a soup dish is eaten with the soup spoon. If you want to get the last bit of it, there is no impropriety in tipping the dish away from you in order to collect it at the edge. Indeed you are paying a subtle compliment to your hostess by thus demonstrating how good it is.

—Eleanor Roosevelt (1884–1962)

Masala Vegetable Stew

An adaptable medley of mixed vegetables in a curried broth

6 to 8 servings

This hearty curry becomes the centerpiece of a satisfying meal served over hot cooked grains, and accompanied by Chapatis (page 158) and a simple, palate-cooling salad of cucumbers and tomatoes.

2 tablespoons olive oil

1 medium onion, chopped

2 to 3 cloves garlic, minced

2 cups baby carrots

2 cups water

1 medium eggplant, peeled and diced

2 medium potatoes, scrubbed and diced

1 large green or red bell pepper, diced

One 16-ounce can salt-free stewed or diced
    tomatoes, undrained

1 to 2 teaspoons grated fresh ginger, to taste

1 to 2 fresh chilies, seeded and minced,
    to taste (see Note)

1 to 2 teaspoons garam masala or good-
    quality curry powder, to taste

1 cup frozen green peas, thawed

¼ cup chopped fresh cilantro, optional

Salt to taste

Hot cooked basmati rice or couscous,
    optional

Per serving:
Calories: 148   Total fat: 4 g   Protein: 5 g   Fiber: 7 g
Carbohydrate: 26 g   Cholesterol: 0 mg   Sodium: 48 mg

Heat the oil in a soup pot and add the onion, garlic, and carrots. Sauté over medium-low heat until the onion is golden, stirring frequently, about 10 minutes.

Add the water, eggplant, potatoes, bell pepper, tomatoes, ginger, chilies, and garam masala. Bring to a rapid simmer, then lower the heat. Cover and simmer gently for 20 to 25 minutes, or until the vegetables are tender but not overdone.

Stir in the peas and cilantro and season with salt. Taste for spiciness and adjust the seasonings as desired. Mash some of the potato dice with a wooden spoon to thicken the cooking liquid. Simmer over low heat, uncovered, for an additional 5 to 10 minutes. The vegetables should be enveloped in a thick liquid.

Serve at once, or if time allows, let the soup stand off the heat for an hour or so, then heat through before serving. Serve in bowls alone or over hot cooked grains.

NOTE:
For a milder flavor, use one 4-ounce can chopped mild green chilies instead of fresh.

VARIATION:
You may substitute other vegetables for the ones listed here. Instead of eggplant, try substituting a medium head of cauliflower, chopped into bite-sized pieces, or use corn kernels in place of the peas. Sweet potato may be used in place of white potato.

Country Captain Stew
A mildly curried vegetable mélange with apples and tofu

6 servings

Though undoubtedly Indian influenced (it bears a passing resemblance to the traditional East Indian mulligatawny soup), this is actually an adaptation of a classic curried chicken stew recipe from the American South.

3 tablespoons olive oil

1 pound firm or extra-firm tofu, blotted and diced

1½ cups chopped onion

3 to 4 cloves garlic, minced

2 cups water

1 large green bell pepper, cut into strips

4 medium potatoes, scrubbed and cut into ½-inch dice

One 16-ounce can salt-free diced tomatoes, undrained

2 Granny Smith apples, peeled, cored, and diced

1 to 2 teaspoons good-quality curry powder, to taste

1 to 2 teaspoons grated fresh ginger, to taste

Pinch of cayenne pepper, optional

½ cup dark raisins

½ cup finely chopped fresh cilantro or parsley

Salt and freshly ground pepper to taste

Vegan Sour Cream (page 7) for garnish, optional

Per serving:
Calories: 333   Total fat: 14 g   Protein: 17 g   Fiber: 7 g
Carbohydrate: 44 g   Cholesterol: 0 mg   Sodium: 25 mg

Heat half of the oil in a large skillet. Add the tofu dice and sauté, stirring frequently, until most sides are golden. Remove from the heat and set aside until needed.

Meanwhile, heat the remaining oil in a soup pot. Add the onion and garlic and sauté over medium-low heat, stirring occasionally, until the onion is golden.

Add the water, bell pepper, potatoes, tomatoes, apples, curry powder, ginger, and optional cayenne pepper. Bring to a rapid simmer, then lower the heat. Cover and simmer gently for about 20 minutes, or until the potatoes are done.

Stir in the sautéed tofu, raisins, and cilantro. Add a little more water if needed, but let the stew remain thick. Season with salt and pepper.

Cook over very low heat for another 10 to 15 minutes. Serve at once or make ahead and reheat when needed. Top each serving with a dollop of sour cream, if desired.

Spanish Vegetable Stew

A wine-scented stew of potatoes, mushrooms, asparagus, and artichokes

6 servings

This classic stew, *menestra de verduras*, has many regional variations, and can be made with different vegetables according to season. Constant ingredients include potatoes, carrots, and green peas; artichokes are the most characteristic. Fresh artichokes are called for in traditional recipes, but using the canned variety simplifies the process.

2 tablespoons extra-virgin olive oil

1 large onion, quartered and thinly sliced

2 to 3 cloves garlic, minced

2 cups water

½ cup dry white wine

3 large potatoes, peeled and diced

4 medium carrots, peeled and sliced

8 ounces white or crimini mushrooms, stemmed and sliced

1½ teaspoons paprika or Spanish paprika

16 slender asparagus stalks, woody ends trimmed, cut into 1-inch pieces

One 15-ounce can imported artichoke hearts, drained and quartered

1 cup frozen green peas

½ cup chopped fresh parsley or cilantro

Juice of ½ to 1 lemon, to taste

Salt and freshly ground pepper to taste

Per serving:
Calories: 222   Total fat: 5 g   Protein: 7 g   Fiber: 10 g
Carbohydrate: 37 g   Cholesterol: 0 mg   Sodium: 100 mg

Heat the oil in a soup pot. Add the onion and sauté over medium heat until translucent. Add the garlic and continue to sauté until the onion is golden.

Add the water, wine, potatoes, carrots, mushrooms, and paprika. Bring to a rapid simmer, then lower the heat. Cover and simmer gently for 15 to 20 minutes, or until the potatoes and carrots are tender. Add the asparagus and cook over low heat until it is tender but still bright green, about 10 minutes.

Stir in the artichoke hearts, peas, and parsley. Season with lemon juice, salt, and pepper. Cook over low heat for 5 minutes longer. If time allows, let the stew stand off the heat for an hour or so. Heat gently before serving. If the stew is too dense, add just a bit more water, then adjust the seasonings.

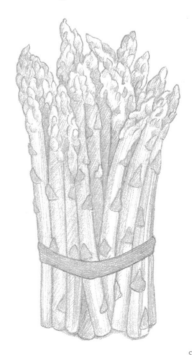

Arborio Rice Soup with Spring Vegetables

Mushroom and asparagus risotto transformed into a thick soup

6 servings

Arborio rice, the same rice used in risotto, makes a comforting base for a spring soup, perfect for drizzly spring evenings.

1 tablespoon olive oil

1 medium onion, finely chopped

2 to 3 cloves garlic, minced

One 32-ounce carton low-sodium
    vegetable broth

4 cups water

¾ cup raw arborio rice

8 to 10 ounces crimini or baby bella
    mushrooms

1 teaspoon dried basil

2 cups slender asparagus stalks, cut into
    ½-inch lengths

1 cup fresh or thawed frozen green peas

1 cup diced fresh tomatoes

¼ to ½ cup minced fresh parsley

¼ cup sliced oil-cured sun-dried tomatoes

Salt and freshly ground pepper to taste

Per serving:
Calories: 197   Total fat: 4 g   Protein: 7 g   Fiber: 5 g
Carbohydrate: 34 g   Cholesterol: 0 mg   Sodium: 290 mg

Heat the oil in a soup pot. Add the onion and garlic and sauté over medium-low heat until both are golden.

Add the broth, 2 cups of the water, rice, mushrooms, and basil. Bring to a rapid simmer, then lower the heat. Cover and simmer gently for 15 to 20 minutes, stirring occasionally, or until the rice is tender.

Stir in the asparagus and remaining 2 cups water. Cover and cook for 5 minutes longer.

Add the peas, tomatoes, parsley, and dried tomatoes. Heat through, and add more water as needed to give the soup a thick but still soupy consistency. Season with salt and pepper and serve.

Red Bean Puree with Zucchini
and lots of herbs and spices

6 to 8 servings

This is a good transitional soup for spring; it's hearty like winter soups, but boasts the fresh flavors of zucchini, parsley, and dill. Taste often to adjust the myriad of flavors to your liking. Consider making any of the muffins on pages 149 to 151 to serve with the soup.

2 tablespoons extra-virgin olive oil

1 large onion, chopped

2 cloves garlic, minced

Two 16-ounce cans small red beans, drained and rinsed, or 4 cups well-cooked small red beans (about 1⅔ cups dried)

4 cups water or cooking liquid from beans

¼ cup dry white wine

2 teaspoons paprika

2 teaspoons ground cumin

1 teaspoon chili powder, or more to taste

1 medium zucchini, quartered lengthwise and cut into ¼-inch slices

¼ cup chopped fresh parsley or cilantro, or more to taste

¼ cup chopped fresh dill

Juice of ½ to 1 lemon or lime, to taste

Salt and freshly ground pepper to taste

Per serving:
Calories: 180   Total fat: 4 g   Protein: 11 g   Fiber: 9 g
Carbohydrate: 31 g   Cholesterol: 0 mg   Sodium: 232 mg

Heat 1 tablespoon of the oil in a soup pot. Add the onion and sauté over medium-low heat until translucent. Add the garlic and continue to sauté until both are lightly browned.

Transfer the onion and garlic to a food processor with about half of the beans and ½ cup of the water. Process until smoothly pureed, then transfer back to the pot. Or add half of the beans and ½ cup of the water to the pot, insert an immersion blender, and process until smoothly pureed.

Stir in the remaining 3½ cups water, remaining beans, wine, paprika, cumin, and chili powder. Bring to a rapid simmer, then lower the heat. Cover and simmer gently for 10 minutes.

Meanwhile, heat the remaining 1 tablespoon of oil in a medium skillet. Add the zucchini and sauté over medium heat, stirring frequently, until some of the pieces are lightly touched with brown. Stir into the soup, followed by the parsley and dill.

Adjust the consistency with enough water to give the soup a slightly thick consistency. Return to a simmer, then season with lemon juice, salt, and pepper. Simmer very gently for 10 minutes longer. If time allows, let the soup stand off the heat for an hour or two, then heat through before serving.

Tomato-Rice Soup
with snow peas and mushrooms

6 to 8 servings

Crisp green snow peas lend this soup a pleasant visual and textural twist.

2 tablespoons olive oil

1 large onion, chopped

4 cups water with 2 vegetable bouillon cubes, or other stock option (page 9)

⅔ cup raw brown rice, rinsed

2 large celery stalks, diced

One 28-ounce can salt-free tomato puree

2 bay leaves

2 teaspoons Italian herb seasoning

8 ounces sliced mushrooms, any variety, or a mixture of two kinds (try baby bellas with shiitakes)

3 to 4 tablespoons chopped fresh parsley

Salt and freshly ground pepper to taste

6 ounces snow peas, trimmed and cut into 1-inch pieces

Per serving:
Calories: 177   Total fat: 5 g   Protein: 6 g   Fiber: 5 g
Carbohydrate: 29 g   Cholesterol: 0 mg   Sodium: 98 mg

Heat the oil in a soup pot. Add the onion and sauté over medium heat until golden.

Add the water with bouillon cubes, rice, celery, tomato puree, bay leaves, and seasoning. Bring to a rapid simmer, then lower the heat. Cover and simmer gently, covered, until the rice is just done, about 40 minutes.

Stir in the mushrooms and parsley and adjust the consistency with enough additional water to give the soup a thick but fluid consistency. Simmer over low heat for another 15 minutes. Season with salt and pepper, then remove from the heat. Discard the bay leaves.

If time allows, let the soup stand off the heat for an hour or so. If the soup becomes too thick, stir in additional water, but let it remain fairly thick. Adjust the seasonings, then heat through.

Just before serving, steam the snow peas until bright green and tender-crisp. After ladling the soup into bowls, garnish each serving with some snow peas.

Creole Lima Bean Stew

with kidney beans and Southern seasonings

6 to 8 servings

Just the thing to serve on a chilly early spring day. Green Chili Cornbread (page 145) or fresh store-bought cornbread would both team well with these flavors.

1 tablespoon olive oil

1 large onion, quartered and thinly sliced

3 celery stalks, thinly sliced

1 large green or red bell pepper, diced

2 tablespoons unbleached white flour

2 cups water

Two 10-ounce packages frozen baby
  lima beans, thawed

One 16-ounce can red kidney beans,
  drained and rinsed

One 28-ounce can salt-free diced tomatoes,
  undrained

2 teaspoons salt-free seasoning
  (see page 4 for brands)

2 bay leaves

½ teaspoon dried basil

½ teaspoon dried thyme

¼ teaspoon dried hot red pepper flakes or
  pinch of cayenne pepper, more or less
  to taste

Salt and freshly ground pepper to taste

¼ to ½ cup chopped fresh parsley

Hot cooked rice, optional

Per serving:
Calories: 220   Total fat: 3 g   Protein: 12 g   Fiber: 10 g
Carbohydrate: 42 g   Cholesterol: 0 mg   Sodium: 161 mg

Heat the oil in a large soup pot. Add the onion and sauté over medium heat until translucent. Add the celery and bell pepper and sauté for another 5 minutes.

Slowly sprinkle in the flour and stir until well integrated with the vegetables, then stir in the water.

Add all the remaining ingredients except the salt and pepper, parsley, and optional rice. Bring to a rapid simmer, then lower the heat. Cover and simmer gently for 30 to 35 minutes.

Season with salt and pepper, then stir in the parsley. Add a small amount of additional water if needed, but let the stew remain thick. Adjust the other seasonings if needed. Discard the bay leaves.

Serve at once, or allow to stand off the heat for an hour or two, then heat through before serving. Serve in bowls over hot cooked rice, if desired.

To make nutritious, healthful, and palatable soup, with flavors properly commingled, is an art which requires study and practice, but it is surprising from what a scant allotment of material a delicate and appetizing dish may be produced.

—The Buckeye Cookbook, 1883

Creole Eggplant Soup
A pleasantly seasoned potage in a creamy base

6 servings

This soup was a favorite discovery of mine while traveling through New Orleans and across the American South many years ago. It's still a soup I love to make when in the mood for eggplant.

2 tablespoons olive oil

1 large onion, chopped

3 medium celery stalks, diced

1 clove garlic, minced

1½ tablespoons unbleached white flour

2 large potatoes, peeled and finely diced

1 large or 2 medium eggplants (1½ pounds total), peeled and finely diced

1 teaspoon dried basil

¼ teaspoon dried thyme

1 teaspoon good-quality curry powder, or more to taste

2 to 3 tablespoons chopped fresh parsley

1 cup rice milk, or more as needed

¼ cup Silk creamer

Salt and freshly ground pepper to taste

Per serving:
Calories: 144   Total fat: 6 g   Protein: 2 g   Fiber: 2 g
Carbohydrate: 21 g   Cholesterol: 0 mg   Sodium: 45 mg

Heat the oil in a large soup pot. Add the onion, celery, and garlic and sauté over medium-low heat, stirring frequently, for 10 minutes, or until all are golden. Add a small amount of water if the mixture becomes dry. Sprinkle in the flour and cook, stirring, for another minute.

Add the potato and eggplant dice with enough water to cover all but about an inch of the vegetables. Bring to a rapid simmer. At this point you should be able to push all the vegetables below the water. Lower the heat, add the basil, thyme, and curry, and stir well. Cover and simmer gently for 30 minutes, or until the vegetables are quite tender.

Stir in the parsley and enough rice milk to give the soup a slightly thick consistency. Stir in the creamer, then season with salt and pepper.

Simmer over very low heat for 5 to 10 minutes longer. Serve at once, or if time allows, let the soup stand off the heat for an hour or so, then heat through before serving.

Okra-Rice Gumbo

A simple rendition of a classic American stew

6 to 8 servings

This standard from the American South contains a varied blend of flavors and textures, all pulled together by the unique character of okra.

2 tablespoons olive oil

2 medium onions, chopped

2 medium celery stalks, diced

5 cups water

One 16-ounce can salt-free diced tomatoes, undrained

4 cups small, tender okra, sliced ½ inch thick

1 medium green bell pepper, chopped

⅔ cup raw brown rice, rinsed

2 bay leaves

1½ teaspoons salt-free seasoning (see page 4 for brands)

¼ teaspoon dried hot red pepper flakes or cayenne pepper, or to taste

Salt and freshly ground pepper to taste

Per serving:
Calories: 153   Total fat: 5 g   Protein: 4 g   Fiber: 5 g
Carbohydrate: 25 g   Cholesterol: 0 mg   Sodium: 28 mg

Heat the oil in a soup pot. Add the onions and celery and sauté over low heat until the onions are golden.

Add the water and all the remaining ingredients except the salt and pepper. Enough red pepper flakes or cayenne should be used to give the soup a distinct bite, but use your discretion. Bring to a simmer, then simmer gently, covered, stirring occasionally, for about an hour, or until the rice is cooked and the vegetables are tender.

Discard the bay leaves and season with salt and pepper. Serve at once, or if time allows, let the soup stand off the heat for an hour or so, then heat through before serving. The soup will thicken considerably as it stands. Add more water as needed and adjust the seasonings, but let it remain very thick.

The great dish of New Orleans, and which it claims the honor of having invented, is the Gumbo. There is no dish which at the same time so tickles the palate, satisfies the appetite, furnishes the body with nutriment sufficient to carry on the physical requirements, and costs so little, as the Creole Gumbo. It is a dinner in itself, being soup, pièce de résistance and vegetable in one. Healthy, not heating to the stomach, and easy of digestion, it should grace every table.

—William Coleman, 1885

Thai-Flavored Coconut Vegetable Soup

Broccoli, carrots, cabbage, mushrooms, and more, mingled in coconut milk

6 or more servings

As in many Asian-style soups, this ingredient list may look long, but it's a snap to prepare. Adding any of the optional ingredients gives this soup a deeper and more authentic flavor.

1 tablespoon olive oil

1 medium onion, quartered and thinly sliced

2 to 3 cloves garlic, minced

2 cups water

Two 13.5-ounce cans light coconut milk

2 medium carrots, sliced diagonally

2 cups broccoli, cut into small florets

2 cups coarsely shredded napa or
green cabbage

8 to 10 ounces white, baby bella, or crimini
mushrooms, sliced

2 teaspoons minced fresh ginger

Juice of ½ to 1 lime, to taste

1 tablespoon natural granulated sugar

Salt to taste

3 scallions, cut into ½-inch lengths

Optional additions (use any or all):

1 teaspoon red or green curry paste, or
to taste

2 stalks lemongrass, cut into thirds and
bruised in several places

¼ cup minced fresh cilantro leaves

Per serving:
Calories: 158   Total fat: 11 g   Protein: 2 g   Fiber: 3 g
Carbohydrate: 17 g   Cholesterol: 0 mg   Sodium: 24 mg

Heat the oil in a soup pot. Add the onion and garlic and sauté over medium heat until golden.

Add the water, coconut milk, carrots, broccoli, cabbage, mushrooms, and ginger. Bring to a simmer, then cover and simmer gently for 3 to 5 minutes, until the vegetables are bright and tender-crisp to your liking. Don't overcook!

Stir in the lime juice, sugar, salt, and scallions. Remove from the heat.

Add whichever optional ingredients you'd like, then cover and let stand off the heat for 20 minutes. Taste to adjust the seasonings, including the ginger and sugar, then heat through as needed before serving.

Southeast Asian–Style Vegetable Stew

Broccoli, cauliflower, green beans, and peppers in a rich coconut-peanut base

6 servings

A one-dish meal, spiced with chili peppers and served over noodles.

2 tablespoons cornstarch

1 cup light coconut milk

¼ cup jarred Thai peanut satay sauce

Juice of 1 lime

2 tablespoons natural granulated sugar

3 to 4 ounces fine rice noodles or
    bean-thread noodles

1 tablespoon olive oil

1 medium onion, finely chopped

3 cloves garlic, minced

3 cups bite-sized broccoli florets

3 cups bite-sized cauliflower florets

2 cups fresh slender green beans, trimmed
    and cut in half (see Note)

1 large red bell pepper, cut into narrow strips

1 to 2 fresh chilies, to taste, seeded and
    minced, or dried hot red pepper flakes to
    taste

1 cup water

Garnishes *(optional):*

Chopped peanuts

Sliced scallions

Per serving:

Calories: 208   Total fat: 8 g   Protein: 5 g   Fiber: 5 g
Carbohydrate: 33 g   Cholesterol: 0 mg   Sodium: 62 mg

To make the sauce, combine the cornstarch with just enough water to dissolve in a medium-sized mixing bowl. Whisk until completely dissolved. Add the coconut milk, peanut sauce, lime juice, and sugar, and whisk together until smooth. Set aside.

Cook the noodles according to package directions until *al dente*, then drain and cut into shorter lengths.

While the noodles are cooking, heat the oil in a soup pot. Add the onion and sauté over medium-low heat until translucent. Add the garlic and continue to sauté until both are golden.

Layer the broccoli, cauliflower, green beans, bell pepper, and chilies in the pot without stirring them in. Pour in about 1 cup water. Bring to a rapid simmer (you'll hear it rather than see it), then lower the heat. Cover and cook for 8 to 10 minutes, or until all the vegetables are tender-crisp.

Add the sauce to the soup pot and stir everything together well. Bring to a gentle simmer and cook for 5 to 10 minutes longer, uncovered, or until the sauce has thickened and the vegetables are just a bit more done than tender-crisp.

Place a small amount of noodles in the bottom of each serving bowl and ladle some of the stew over them. If you wish, garnish with chopped peanuts, sliced scallions, or both.

NOTE:

If fresh slender green beans are unavailable, substitute frozen. Try Cascadian Farms organic petite whole green beans for a nice effect.

Chinese Cabbage and Tofu Soup

An easy and tasty rendition of the Asian restaurant classic

4 to 6 servings

This light soup, served with Scallion Pancakes (page 157), is a great introduction to Asian-style vegetable stir-fries.

1 tablespoon olive oil

1 large onion, quartered and thinly sliced

2 cups firmly packed, finely shredded napa or savoy cabbage

¾ cup thinly sliced small white mushrooms

One 6-ounce can sliced water chestnuts, undrained

One 32-ounce carton low-sodium vegetable broth, or 1 recipe Asian Mushroom Broth (page 15)

2 tablespoons dry sherry or red wine

2 teaspoons reduced-sodium soy sauce

Freshly ground pepper to taste

1 cup snow peas, trimmed and halved

8 ounces soft or firm tofu, cut into ½-inch dice

Per serving:
Calories: 117   Total fat: 5 g   Protein: 5 g   Fiber: 4 g
Carbohydrate: 14 g   Cholesterol: 0 mg   Sodium: 415 mg

Heat the oil in a large soup pot. Add the onion and sauté over low heat until golden.

Add the remaining ingredients except the snow peas and tofu. Bring to a rapid simmer, then lower the heat. Cover and simmer over low heat for 10 minutes.

Remove from the heat. Stir in the snow peas and tofu and let the soup stand for 30 minutes. Heat through and serve at once.

Good manners: The noise you don't make when you're eating soup.

—Bennett Cerf (1898–1971)

Gingery Miso-Spinach Soup
with baby corn and tofu

4 to 6 servings

Simple, quick, and colorful, this soup is best eaten as soon as it is done. It makes a nice introduction to Asian rice or noodle dishes.

1 tablespoon olive oil

1 small onion or 2 to 3 shallot sections, minced

1 medium carrot, peeled and sliced

4 cups water with 2 vegetable bouillon cubes, or other stock option (page 9)

6 to 8 ounces fresh spinach or baby spinach, well washed, stemmed, and coarsely chopped

3 scallions, white and green parts, sliced

2 to 3 tablespoons dry white or red wine, optional

2 teaspoons minced fresh ginger, or more to taste

Freshly ground pepper to taste

4 ounces soft or firm tofu, cut into ½-inch dice

One 15-ounce can cut baby corn, undrained

2 to 4 tablespoons miso, any variety, to taste

Per serving:
Calories: 92   Total fat: 5 g   Protein: 5 g   Fiber: 5 g
Carbohydrate: 9 g   Cholesterol: 0 mg   Sodium: 565 mg

Heat the oil in a soup pot. Add the onion and carrot and sauté over medium-low heat until both are golden, stirring frequently.

Add the water with bouillon cubes, spinach, scallions, optional wine, ginger, and pepper. Bring to a rapid simmer, then lower the heat. Cover and simmer very gently for 10 minutes. Add the tofu and baby corn with its liquid.

Dissolve the miso in enough water to make it smooth and pourable. Stir into the soup. If the soup is too dense, add more water as needed and heat through very gently. Serve at once.

Asian Noodle Soup with a Myriad of Mushrooms
and lots of scallions

6 servings

This Asian-style soup is a treat for mushroom aficionados. Scallion Pancakes (page 157) are a good accompaniment. This is a perfect introduction to a simple meal of stir-fried vegetables with tofu.

1 recipe Asian Mushroom Broth (page 15), with trimmed shiitake mushrooms

2 teaspoons dark sesame oil

1 clove garlic, minced

4 scallions, white and green parts, sliced

6 to 8 ounces fresh mushrooms, any variety, cleaned and sliced

One 15-ounce can Asian mushrooms, such as straw, abalone, or oyster mushrooms (leave straw mushrooms whole; coarsely chop abalone or oyster), undrained

One 6-ounce can sliced water chestnuts, undrained

1 tablespoon rice vinegar

1 tablespoon cornstarch

3 to 4 ounces rice-stick noodles

Reduced-sodium soy sauce to taste

Freshly ground pepper to taste

Per serving:
Calories: 154   Total fat: 4 g   Protein: 4 g   Fiber: 4 g
Carbohydrate: 28 g   Cholesterol: 0 mg   Sodium: 600 mg

Prepare the broth according to the recipe.

Heat the oil in a soup pot, then add the garlic and white parts of the scallions and sauté over medium-low heat for 2 or 3 minutes.

Add the broth, green parts of the scallions, fresh mushrooms, canned mushrooms with liquid, water chestnuts with liquid, and rice vinegar. Bring to a rapid simmer, then lower the heat. Cover and simmer gently for 10 minutes.

Dissolve the cornstarch in just enough water to make it pourable, and stir into the soup. Break up the rice-stick noodles and add them to the soup. Simmer for 5 minutes, or until the noodles are *al dente*.

Season with soy sauce and pepper, and adjust the consistency with water if the soup is too dense. Serve at once.

Mixed Mushroom Soup with Bok Choy

An aromatic broth featuring portabellas and crunchy greens

4 to 6 servings

This aromatic, brothy soup celebrates the spring arrival of fresh bok choy, a favorite Asian green vegetable. This is an excellent way to whet the appetite for an Asian-style vegetable stir-fry with rice or noodles.

1 recipe Asian Mushroom Broth (page 15), with trimmed shiitake mushrooms

1½ cups sliced small white, crimini, or baby bella mushrooms

2 fresh portabella mushrooms, about 4 inches in diameter, thinly sliced, then cut into bite-sized pieces

¼ cup dry white wine, optional

5 to 6 stalks bok choy, greens included, thinly sliced

3 to 4 scallions, white and green parts, sliced

2 to 3 tablespoons reduced-sodium soy sauce, to taste

Freshly ground pepper to taste

Per serving:
Calories: 90   Total fat: 2 g   Protein: 4 g   Fiber: 4 g
Carbohydrate: 14 g   Cholesterol: 0 mg   Sodium: 628 mg

Prepare the broth according to the recipe.

Once done, add the two other kinds of mushrooms to the broth, then stir in the optional wine. Bring to a rapid simmer, then lower the heat. Cover and simmer gently for 10 to 15 minutes, or until the mushrooms are done but still pleasantly chewy.

Add the remaining ingredients and simmer for 5 to 8 minutes longer, or just until the bok choy is tender-crisp. Serve at once.

I am a mushroom
On whom the dew of heaven
Drops now and then.

—John Ford
    The Broken Heart, 1633

Japanese Soba Noodle Soup
with tofu and spring greens

6 servings

Serve this soup Asian-style. Slurp the noodles from the broth with chopsticks, then use an Asian soup spoon to scoop up what's left. This simple soup comes together in less than 30 minutes.

One 8-ounce package soba
   (buckwheat noodles)
One 32-ounce carton low-sodium
   vegetable broth
6 to 8 medium-sized shiitake mushroom
   caps, sliced
2 tablespoons reduced-sodium soy sauce, or
   more to taste
2 teaspoons rice vinegar
2 teaspoons natural granulated sugar
2 to 3 teaspoons minced fresh ginger,
   to taste
3 scallions, white and green parts, thinly
   sliced
8 ounces soft or firm tofu
8 to 10 ounces fresh spinach, well washed,
   stemmed, and chopped
1 cup chopped baby bok choy, tatsoi, or
   mizuna, optional
Freshly ground pepper to taste

Per serving:
Calories: 196   Total fat: 3 g   Protein: 10 g   Fiber: 3 g
Carbohydrate: 33 g   Cholesterol: 0 mg   Sodium: 511 mg

Break the noodles in half and cook them in a large saucepan according to package directions until *al dente*, then drain. Rinse briefly with cool water.

Meanwhile, combine the broth, mushrooms, soy sauce, vinegar, sugar, and ginger in a soup pot. Bring to a rapid simmer, then lower the heat. Cover and simmer gently for 10 minutes.

Stir in the scallions, tofu, spinach, and optional bok choy. Cover and cook until the spinach is wilted but still bright green, about 3 minutes.

Stir in the noodles. Add about 2 cups water, or enough to give the soup a dense but not overly crowded consistency. Season with pepper and additional soy sauce if needed. Heat through and serve at once.

Sushi Soup

A surprising presentation of rice, nori, and uncooked vegetables

6 to 8 servings

I'm a big fan of vegetable sushi, so I thought it would be fun to concoct a soup that featured all of its flavors and textures, without all the work of rolling and cutting. The result is an offbeat, rice- and nori-filled broth topped with colorful raw veggies.

1 cup raw short-grain brown rice, rinsed

2¼ cups water

2 tablespoons rice vinegar

1 tablespoon natural granulated sugar

2 sheets pretoasted nori

One 32-ounce carton low-sodium
   vegetable broth

2 tablespoons reduced-sodium soy sauce,
   or to taste

2 to 3 good handfuls of baby spinach or
   watercress leaves, coarsely shredded

Toppings (choose 3):

1 medium carrot, peeled and grated

½ medium cucumber, peeled, seeded,
   and cut into matchsticks or grated

1 medium avocado, finely diced

½ cup fresh shiitake mushrooms, sliced
   and steamed

½ cup peeled, grated daikon radish

Per serving:
Calories: 123   Total fat: 1 g   Protein: 3 g   Fiber: 2 g
Carbohydrate: 26 g   Cholesterol: 0 mg   Sodium: 365 mg

Combine the rice with the water in a soup pot. Bring to a boil, then lower the heat. Cover and cook until the water is absorbed, about 30 minutes. Test to see if the rice is tender; if it needs a bit more cooking, add ½ cup water and simmer, uncovered, until absorbed.

Once the rice is cooked, add the vinegar and sugar and stir well to combine. Allow to stand, uncovered, for a few minutes.

Using kitchen shears, cut the nori into short, narrow strips, about ½ by 1½ inches.

Pour the broth over the rice, then stir in the nori and soy sauce. Bring to a rapid simmer, then remove from the heat, cover, and let stand while preparing the toppings of your choice.

Serve the soup as follows: Ladle the soup into bowls, filling them about three-quarters full. Place a small amount of spinach leaves atop each serving, then arrange a small pile of each of your 3 selected toppings over the greens. Serve at once.

Summer

When the appetite is dulled by summer's heat, nothing is more appealing than a bowl of refreshing cold soup. These soups make lavish use of garden vegetables, lush fruits, and fresh herbs. For really lazy, languid days, you'll find a number of soups that require no cooking at all.

Cream of Green Pea and Cucumber Soup
A cool green puree with a hint of dill and lime

6 servings

This brightly colored soup makes a delightful introduction to a summer dinner, or it can be the centerpiece of a light meal accompanied by salad-filled wraps.

1½ tablespoons olive oil

1 cup chopped onion

3 cloves garlic, minced

2 large potatoes, peeled and diced

2 cups frozen green peas, thawed

¼ cup chopped fresh parsley

2 tablespoons chopped fresh dill

1½ cups rice milk, more or less as needed

Juice of 1 lime, or to taste

Salt and freshly ground pepper to taste

1 cup fresh or frozen green peas, steamed
    until just done

1 large cucumber, peeled, seeded, and
    coarsely grated or finely diced

Per serving:
Calories: 166   Total fat: 4 g   Protein: 5 g   Fiber: 4 g
Carbohydrate: 29 g   Cholesterol: 0 mg   Sodium: 83 mg

Heat the oil in a soup pot. Add the onion and sauté over medium-low heat until translucent. Add the garlic and continue to sauté until both are golden.

Add the potatoes and just enough water to cover all but about ½ inch of the vegetables. Bring to a rapid simmer, then lower the heat. Cover and simmer gently until the vegetables are tender, about 20 minutes.

Stir in the peas, parsley, and dill, and simmer for 2 to 3 minutes longer.

Transfer the solid ingredients to a food processor. Process in batches until smoothly pureed or leave a little texture, as you prefer. Transfer back to the soup pot. Or insert an immersion blender into the soup pot and process until the vegetables are pureed to your liking.

Stir in enough rice milk to give the soup a slightly thick consistency. Season with lime juice, salt, and pepper. Remove from the heat and let the soup cool to room temperature.

Just before serving, stir in the steamed peas and grated cucumber. Serve at room temperature or refrigerate for an hour or two and serve chilled.

VARIATION:
For a richer soup, whisk in ¼ cup raw or toasted cashew butter just after removing the soup from the heat.

Cool Ratatouille

The classic mélange of eggplant, zucchini, and tomatoes

6 to 8 servings

This summery version of the classic stew makes use of summer's lush tomatoes and fresh herbs. Serve with slices of fresh whole-grain baguette or olive bread.

2 tablespoons extra-virgin olive oil

1 large red onion, chopped

3 to 4 cloves garlic, minced

1 cup water

2 medium eggplants (about 1½ pounds total), peeled and diced

2 small zucchini, sliced

4 cups diced ripe, juicy, fresh tomatoes

1 cup sliced baby bella or crimini mushrooms

1 cup salt-free tomato sauce

¼ cup dry red wine

1 teaspoon paprika

¼ cup thinly sliced fresh basil leaves, or more to taste

¼ cup chopped fresh parsley

1 tablespoon fresh oregano leaves, or more to taste

2 teaspoons fresh thyme leaves, or more to taste

Salt and freshly ground pepper to taste

Vegan Sour Cream (page 7) for garnish, optional

Per serving:
Calories: 109   Total fat: 4 g   Protein: 3 g   Fiber: 5 g
Carbohydrate: 16 g   Cholesterol: 0 mg   Sodium: 18 mg

Heat the oil in a large soup pot. Add the onion and garlic and sauté over medium heat until both are golden, about 8 to 10 minutes.

Add the water, eggplant, zucchini, tomatoes, mushrooms, tomato sauce, wine, and paprika. Bring to a rapid simmer, then lower the heat. Cover and simmer gently until the vegetables are tender but not overdone, about 25 to 30 minutes. Stir occasionally, making sure there is enough liquid for the vegetables to simmer in without being too soupy.

Remove from the heat. Stir in half of the basil and the remaining fresh herbs. Season with salt and pepper. Let the stew cool to room temperature.

To serve, garnish each serving with the remaining basil strips and, if desired, a dollop of sour cream.

It is not an exaggeration to say that peace and happiness begin, geographically, where garlic is used in cooking.

—X. Marcel Boulestin (1878–1943)

Late-Summer Eggplant Stew
with pasta, dried tomatoes, and olives

6 to 8 servings

Try this Mediterranean-inspired stew with fresh corn on the cob; a salad of mixed baby greens, colorful bell peppers, and mushrooms; and some crusty bread spread with hummus.

2 tablespoons extra-virgin olive oil

1 medium onion, quartered and thinly sliced

2 to 3 cloves garlic, pressed or minced

3 cups water

2 medium eggplants (about 1½ pounds total), peeled and cut into ½-inch dice

1 cup small pasta, such as tiny shells or cut fusilli

4 cups diced ripe tomatoes (try a mixture of red and yellow tomatoes)

½ cup finely chopped fresh parsley

1 tablespoon fresh oregano leaves, or 1 teaspoon dried

½ cup coarsely chopped cured black olives

½ cup oil-cured sun-dried tomatoes, sliced

Salt and freshly ground pepper to taste

8 to 12 fresh basil leaves, cut into strips

Per serving:
Calories: 187   Total fat: 8 g   Protein: 5 g   Fiber: 8 g
Carbohydrate: 27 g   Cholesterol: 0 mg   Sodium: 146 mg

Heat the oil in a soup pot. Add the onion and garlic and sauté over medium-low heat until the onion is golden.

Add the water and eggplant. Bring to a rapid simmer, then lower the heat. Cover and simmer gently until the eggplant is just tender, about 15 minutes.

Meanwhile, in a separate large saucepan, cook the pasta until *al dente*, then drain.

Stir the tomatoes, half of the parsley, and the oregano into the soup pot. Return to a gentle simmer, then cook for 5 to 10 minutes longer, or until the eggplant is completely tender.

Stir in the olives, dried tomatoes, and cooked pasta. Season with salt and pepper. Remove from the heat and let the stew stand for an hour or so, uncovered.

Adjust the consistency with more water as needed for a thick but still fluid consistency. Adjust the seasonings. Serve just warm or at room temperature. Garnish each serving with a sprinkling of the remaining parsley and a few strips of basil.

Summer Garden Pasta Soup
Tomatoes, zucchini, and little shells in a light broth

6 to 8 servings

This garden-fresh medley is a good choice when you want a summery soup that is slightly warm rather than chilled.

6 cups water with 2 vegetable bouillon cubes, or other stock option (page 9)

2 pounds ripe tomatoes, diced

¼ cup oil-cured sun-dried tomatoes, finely diced

2 medium-small zucchini, quartered lengthwise and sliced

3 to 4 scallions, white and green parts, thinly sliced

One 16-ounce can navy beans, drained and rinsed

¼ to ½ cup chopped fresh parsley, to taste

Salt and freshly ground pepper to taste

2 cups tiny shell pasta or ditalini

Per serving:
Calories: 230 Total fat: 3 g Protein: 11 g Fiber: 6 g
Carbohydrate: 42 g Cholesterol: 0 mg Sodium: 275 mg

Combine the water with bouillon cubes in a large soup pot with the fresh and dried tomatoes, zucchini, and scallions. Bring to a rapid simmer, then lower the heat. Cover and simmer gently until the zucchini is tender but still firm, about 10 minutes.

Add the beans and parsley, then season with salt and pepper. Remove from the heat and let the soup stand off the heat for an hour or so before serving. This will give it time to cool somewhat as well as to develop flavor.

About 20 minutes before the soup is to be served, bring water to boil in a separate large saucepan and cook the pasta until *al dente*. Drain and rinse briefly with cool water, then stir into the soup. Taste to adjust the salt and pepper, then serve just warm.

Tangy Potato-Spinach Soup
A compatible pair of vegetables in a cool, creamy base

6 to 8 servings

Here's a cold soup that is substantial as well as refreshing. Serve with a fresh flatbread and tabbouleh salad.

5 to 6 medium potatoes, peeled and diced
1 small onion, cut in half
2 bay leaves
One 32-ounce carton low-sodium
    vegetable broth
12 to 16 ounces fresh spinach, well washed,
    stemmed, and chopped
1 recipe Vegan Sour Cream (page 7)
½ cup Silk creamer
1 cup rice milk, or more as needed
¼ cup chopped fresh parsley
2 tablespoons minced fresh dill
Juice of ½ to 1 lemon, to taste
Salt and freshly ground pepper to taste

Per serving:
Calories: 153   Total fat: 4 g   Protein: 6 g   Fiber: 3 g
Carbohydrate: 27 g   Cholesterol: 0 mg   Sodium: 372 mg

Combine the potatoes, onion, and bay leaves in a large soup pot with the broth. Bring to a simmer, then lower the heat. Cover and simmer gently until the potatoes are tender, about 20 minutes. Remove from the heat. Discard the bay leaves. Remove and set aside the onion halves.

With a slotted spoon, transfer a heaping cup of the potato dice into a small bowl, mash well, and stir back into the soup. Stir in the spinach leaves and cook for another minute or two, just until they are wilted. Remove from the heat.

Combine the sour cream, creamer, and rice milk in a food processor. Add the cooked onion halves and process until smooth. Add the parsley and dill and pulse on and off until they are finely chopped.

Stir the sour cream mixture into the soup pot, then allow the soup to cool to room temperature, uncovered. If needed, thin the soup with additional rice milk, then season with lemon juice, salt, and pepper. Chill thoroughly before serving.

Cool Creamy Potato-Leek Soup
with arugula and a touch of curry

6 to 8 servings

Mild potatoes contrast with the earthy tones of arugula in a lightly curried soup.

2 tablespoons olive oil

2 medium onions, chopped

2 cloves garlic, minced

6 medium potatoes, peeled and diced

2 to 3 medium leeks, white and palest green parts only, chopped and well washed

½ cup finely diced red bell pepper

4 ounces arugula (Use baby arugula leaves whole; chop larger arugula leaves)

1 recipe Vegan Sour Cream (page 7)

1½ cups rice milk, more or less as needed

¼ cup minced fresh parsley or cilantro

1 to 2 teaspoons good-quality curry powder, to taste

Salt and freshly ground pepper to taste

Per serving:
Calories: 204   Total fat: 6 g   Protein: 6 g   Fiber: 3 g
Carbohydrate: 34 g   Cholesterol: 0 mg   Sodium: 134 mg

Heat the oil in a large soup pot. Add the onions and garlic and sauté over medium heat until the onions are golden.

Add the potatoes and enough water to cover all but about ½ inch of the vegetables. Bring to a rapid simmer, then lower the heat. Cover and simmer gently until the potatoes are tender, about 20 minutes. Remove from the heat and let cool to room temperature.

Just before serving, place the leeks in a skillet with about ½ inch of water. Cover and steam the leeks for 5 to 8 minutes, or until wilted, stirring occasionally. Add the red pepper and continue to steam until both vegetables are just tender.

Making sure that the bottom of the skillet is still moist, add the arugula and cover. Cook just until it has wilted down a bit, about 1 to 2 minutes.

With a slotted spoon, transfer the potato-onion mixture to a food processor. Add the sour cream and a little of the rice milk and puree until smooth. Return to the soup pot, then stir in the remaining rice milk. Or if using an immersion blender, add the sour cream and rice milk to the pot with the potato-onion mixture, and puree until smooth.

Stir the leeks and greens mixture into the soup pot. Adjust the consistency with more rice milk, if needed, to give the soup a medium-thick consistency.

Stir in the parsley. Season with curry, salt, and pepper, then serve at room temperature, or cover and chill for an hour or two before serving.

Garden Greens Soup

Leafy veggies and herbs with a sprinkling of couscous

6 servings

A soup that looks and tastes garden-fresh, this is a good one to serve all summer long.

⅓ cup raw couscous, preferably whole-grain

1½ tablespoons olive oil

2 medium onions, quartered and thinly sliced

2 to 3 cloves garlic, minced

4 cups water with 2 vegetable bouillon cubes, or other stock option (page 9)

½ small head napa or savoy cabbage, thinly shredded

5 to 6 ounces fresh spinach, well washed, stemmed, and chopped (see Note)

2 cups shredded lettuce, any dark green variety

2 medium tomatoes, finely diced

¼ cup chopped fresh parsley

2 tablespoons minced fresh dill

3 scallions, white and green parts, thinly sliced

1 teaspoon good-quality curry powder

Juice of ½ lemon

Salt and freshly ground pepper to taste

Per serving:
Calories: 118   Total fat: 5 g   Protein: 4 g   Fiber: 0 g
Carbohydrate: 17 g   Cholesterol: 0 mg   Sodium: 84 mg

Place the couscous in a heatproof container and cover with ⅔ cup boiling water. Cover and let stand until needed.

Heat the oil in a large soup pot. Add the onions and garlic, and sauté over medium-low heat until the onions are golden.

Add the remaining ingredients except the salt and pepper. Bring to a rapid simmer, then lower the heat. Cover and simmer gently for 8 to 10 minutes, or until the vegetables are just tender.

Remove from the heat and stir in the cooked couscous. Adjust the consistency with about 2 cups water, more or less as needed, to give the soup a dense but not overly crowded consistency.

Season with salt and pepper, then allow the soup to cool to room temperature and serve.

NOTE:
If using baby spinach, simply rinse it and pull off any stems that you find too long; no need to chop the leaves.

Cream of Lettuce Soup
with fresh summer herbs

6 servings

Cheddar-Oat Griddle Biscuits (page 153) provide a nice contrast to the mild flavor of this pleasant summer soup. Or try it with Garlic Croutons (page 159), if you'd prefer a little crunch.

1½ tablespoons olive oil

2 medium onions, chopped

3 to 4 cloves garlic, minced

2 ½ cups water with 1 vegetable bouillon cube, or other stock option (page 9)

10 cups coarsely chopped tender green lettuce such as Boston or bibb

½ cup minced fresh herbs (choose from a mixture of chives, dill, oregano, basil, and parsley)

One 12.3-ounce package firm silken tofu, or one 16-ounce can cannellini beans, drained and rinsed

1 to 2 cups rice milk, or as needed

Juice of ½ lemon, or more to taste

Salt and freshly ground pepper to taste

Vegan Sour Cream (page 7), optional

Per serving:
Calories: 122   Total fat: 6 g   Protein: 6 g   Fiber: 2 g
Carbohydrate: 12 g   Cholesterol: 0 mg   Sodium: 68 mg

Heat the oil in a soup pot. Add the onions and garlic and sauté over medium-low heat until the onions are lightly browned.

Add the water with bouillon cube and 8 cups of the lettuce, reserving the rest. Bring to a rapid simmer, then lower the heat. Cover and simmer gently for 10 minutes. Stir in the herbs and remove from the heat.

With a slotted spoon, transfer the solid ingredients to a food processor along with the tofu, and puree, in batches, if necessary, until smooth. Or add the tofu to the soup pot, insert an immersion blender, and puree until smooth.

Return to the soup pot or to a serving container. Stir in enough rice milk to give the soup a slightly thick consistency. Season with lemon juice, salt, and pepper. This soup needs a good amount of each to bring up the flavor, so be generous yet judicious.

Cut the reserved lettuce into fine shreds and stir in. Allow to cool to room temperature. Serve at room temperature or chill the soup in the refrigerator for at least an hour before serving. Top each serving with a dollop of sour cream, if desired.

Cool as a Cucumber Soup
with lots of fresh herbs in a sour cream base

4 to 6 servings

Here's an exceptionally easy, no-cook soup. This evolved from the classic recipe for Middle Eastern cucumber soup, which is made with a base of yogurt. However, I don't think it tastes right with soy yogurt, so I tinkered with it until it approximated the original flavor, without the yogurt. I enjoy it with barley added, as suggested in the variation below.

2 large cucumbers, peeled and seeded

1 recipe Vegan Sour Cream (page 7)

½ cup finely chopped mixed fresh herbs
   (such as dill, parsley, and mint),
   or more to taste

1 to 2 scallions, green parts only, thinly sliced

1½ cups rice milk, or as needed

Juice of ½ lemon, or more to taste

½ teaspoon ground cumin, or more to taste

Salt and freshly ground pepper to taste

Per serving:
Calories: 88   Total fat: 2 g   Protein: 5 g   Fiber: 1 g
Carbohydrate: 14 g   Cholesterol: 0 mg   Sodium: 166 mg

Grate the cucumbers on a coarse grater, either by hand or in a food processor fitted with the grating disk.

Transfer the cucumbers to a serving container. Stir in the sour cream, herbs, scallions, and enough rice milk to give the soup a slightly thick consistency. Season with lemon juice, cumin, salt, and pepper. Serve at once or refrigerate until well chilled.

VARIATIONS:

For a heartier version of this soup, add a cup or so of cold, cooked barley.

For a pleasantly peppery flavor, stir in a good handful of chopped watercress leaves.

Tomato-Mango Coconut Cooler
Summer veggies with a Thai twist

6 servings

Think of this no-cook soup as a Thai-flavored gazpacho. It's best with really lush summer tomatoes. Serve with a cold noodle dish for a quick summer meal.

4 medium ripe tomatoes, finely diced
1 ripe mango, finely diced
½ medium cucumber, peeled, seeded,
    and finely diced
½ medium red bell pepper, finely diced
2 scallions, green parts only, thinly sliced
¼ cup chopped fresh cilantro, or more to
    taste
Two 13.5-ounce cans light coconut milk
1 teaspoon good-quality curry powder
¼ cup jarred Thai peanut satay sauce,
    whisked together with ¼ cup hot water
2 to 3 tablespoons lime juice, to taste
Salt to taste
Chopped peanuts for garnish, optional

Per serving:
Calories: 168   Total fat: 11 g   Protein: 3 g   Fiber: 2 g
Carbohydrate: 19 g   Cholesterol: 0 mg   Sodium: 46 mg

Combine all the ingredients except the last two in a serving container. Cover and refrigerate for an hour or two, until chilled.

Add salt to taste and adjust the other seasonings, if necessary. Serve, topping each serving with a sprinkling of chopped peanuts, if desired.

Cool Curried Zucchini and Carrot Soup

in a white bean and silken tofu base

6 servings

*This refreshing cold soup is one that I often serve
to summer company.*

1 tablespoon olive oil

1 medium onion, quartered and thinly sliced

2 medium carrots, peeled and grated

2 medium zucchini, grated

One 12.3-ounce package firm silken tofu

One 16-ounce can great northern or
    cannellini beans, drained and rinsed

¼ cup minced fresh parsley

3 to 4 cups rice milk, or as needed

2 teaspoons good-quality curry powder

2 tablespoons minced fresh dill

Juice of ½ to 1 lemon, to taste

Salt and freshly ground pepper to taste

Per serving:

Calories: 233   Total fat: 5 g   Protein: 11 g   Fiber: 5 g
Carbohydrate: 37 g   Cholesterol: 0 mg   Sodium: 80 mg

Heat the oil in a medium skillet. Add the onion and sauté over medium-low heat until golden.

Add the carrots and a small amount of water, just enough to keep the bottom of the skillet moist. Cover and cook over medium heat for 3 minutes. Add the zucchini and continue to cook, covered, until the carrots and zucchini are tender but not overdone, about 3 minutes longer. Uncover and set aside until needed.

Combine the tofu, half of the beans, the parsley, and 1 cup of the rice milk in a food processor. Process until smoothly pureed.

Transfer the puree to a serving container. Stir in the carrot and zucchini mixture, the remaining beans, and enough additional rice milk to give the soup a flowing, medium-thick consistency. Stir in the curry powder and dill, then season with lemon juice, salt, and pepper.

Allow the soup to stand for an hour or so to allow the flavors to blend, then serve at room temperature. Or refrigerate the soup for an hour or two and serve chilled.

To dream of carrots signifies strength and profit to them that are at law for an inheritance, for we pluck them out of the ground with our hand.

—Richard Folkard
    Plant Lore, Legends and Lyrics, 1884

Cold Zucchini and Corn Soup
A refreshing summer chowder

6 to 8 servings

Zucchini and corn are an appealing pair. Serve with Garlic Croutons (page 159) to add a pleasant crunch.

2 tablespoons olive oil

1 small onion, chopped

1 clove garlic, minced

2 pounds zucchini, diced

2 cups cooked fresh corn kernels (from about 3 good-sized ears)

One 32-ounce carton low-sodium vegetable broth, or other stock option (page 9)

¼ cup chopped fresh parsley

1 teaspoon ground cumin

2 scallions, green parts only, minced

2 tablespoons finely chopped fresh basil leaves

1 recipe Vegan Sour Cream (page 7)

1 to 2 tablespoons lemon juice, to taste

Salt and freshly ground pepper to taste

Per serving:
Calories: 131   Total fat: 6 g   Protein: 6 g   Fiber: 2 g
Carbohydrate: 17 g   Cholesterol: 0 mg   Sodium: 315 mg

Heat 1 tablespoon of the oil in a soup pot. Add the onion and garlic and sauté over medium-low heat until the onion is golden.

Set aside half of the zucchini dice and half of the corn kernels. Add the remainder to the soup pot along with the broth, parsley, and cumin. Bring to a rapid simmer, then lower the heat. Cover and simmer gently until the zucchini is tender, about 10 minutes.

With a slotted spoon, transfer the solid ingredients to a food processor or blender and puree, in batches if necessary, until smooth. Return to the soup pot, then allow to cool to room temperature.

Heat the remaining tablespoon of oil in a skillet. Add the reserved zucchini and sauté over medium heat until it is just beginning to brown lightly.

Once the soup is cool, stir in the sautéed zucchini, reserved corn kernels, scallions, basil, sour cream, and lemon juice.

If needed, adjust the consistency with enough water to give the soup a dense but not overly crowded consistency. Season with salt and pepper. Serve at room temperature or refrigerate for an hour or two until chilled.

Cream of Corn and Watercress Soup
with a sprinkling of fresh oregano

6 to 8 servings

*The peppery flavor of watercress provides a de-
lightful contrast to the sweetness of summer corn.*

6 medium ears fresh sweet corn
2 tablespoons olive oil
2 large onions, chopped
2 cloves garlic, minced
2 medium potatoes, peeled and diced
2 cups chopped watercress leaves and stems
2 cups rice milk, or as needed
Salt and freshly ground pepper to taste
1 tablespoon fresh oregano leaves,
    or more to taste

Per serving:
Calories: 186   Total fat: 5 g   Protein: 5 g   Fiber: 4 g
Carbohydrate: 35 g   Cholesterol: 0 mg   Sodium: 31 mg

Cook the corn in plenty of rapidly simmering water until
the kernels are just tender. Remove the corn with tongs
and reserve the cooking water. When the corn is cool
enough to handle, scrape the kernels off the cobs with a
sharp knife. Set the kernels aside.

Heat the oil in a soup pot. Add the onions and garlic and
sauté over medium-low heat until both are golden.

Add the potatoes and 4 cups of the cooking liquid
from the corn, and bring to a rapid simmer, then lower
the heat. Cover and simmer gently for 10 minutes. Add
half of the watercress. Simmer until the potatoes are
tender, about 10 to 15 minutes longer, then remove from
the heat.

Set aside a cup of the corn kernels and puree the remainder in a food processor or blender until fairly smooth.
Transfer the puree to a bowl.

With a slotted spoon, transfer the solid ingredients from
the soup to the food processor or blender and puree
until smooth. Return the puree to the soup pot, along
with the corn puree, the reserved corn kernels, and the
reserved watercress.

Return to low heat and stir in enough rice milk to give
the soup a slightly thick consistency. Season with salt
and pepper, then cover and simmer over low heat for
another 10 to 15 minutes. Let the soup cool to room
temperature, then refrigerate until chilled. Top each
serving with a sprinkling of oregano leaves.

"Eat well of the cresses" was a common bit of advice given by Renaissance herbalists, for it was believed that consuming these greens aided the memory.

Corn Puree with Roasted Peppers

and lots of onion and garlic

6 servings

An appetizing soup designed to impress summer guests—or your own family!

6 large ears fresh sweet corn

2 tablespoons light or extra-virgin olive oil

2 large onions, chopped

4 cloves garlic, minced

Pinch of cayenne pepper

1 to 1½ cups rice milk, as needed

Salt and freshly ground pepper to taste

2 large red bell peppers

1 large green bell pepper

6 large fresh basil leaves, sliced into strips, minced fresh parsley, or fresh oregano leaves for garnish

Per serving:
Calories: 230   Total fat: 7 g   Protein: 6 g   Fiber: 7 g
Carbohydrate: 42 g   Cholesterol: 0 mg   Sodium: 40 mg

Cook the corn in plenty of rapidly simmering water until the kernels are just tender. Remove the corn with tongs and reserve the cooking water. When the corn is cool enough to handle, scrape the kernels off the cobs with a sharp knife. Set aside 1 cup of kernels.

Meanwhile, heat the oil in a soup pot. Add the onions and garlic and sauté over medium-low heat until the onions are golden and just beginning to be touched with brown spots. Transfer the onions and garlic to a food processor and process with the corn kernels (except for the reserved cup), in batches if necessary, until smoothly pureed. Transfer back to the soup pot.

Stir in 4 cups of the cooking water from the corn. Bring to a rapid simmer, then add the cayenne pepper and enough rice milk to give the soup a slightly thick consistency. Cover and simmer gently for 10 minutes. Season with salt and pepper. Allow the soup to stand off the heat, uncovered, for about an hour.

Meanwhile, set the bell peppers under the broiler, turning them frequently until the skins are quite blistered and fairly charred. Place the peppers in a brown paper bag and fold shut. Let the peppers cool in the bag for 30 minutes or so, then remove them from the bag, slip the skins off, and remove the stems and seeds. Cut the peppers into narrow strips.

Serve the soup just warm or at room temperature, garnishing each serving with some roasted pepper strips and fresh herb of your choice.

Fresh Tomato Soup with Sweet Corn Sauce

A summer night's visual feast

6 servings

This cold soup is as appealing to look at as it is to eat. Serve with fresh bread and follow with a pasta salad for a light summer meal. Use really lush, ripe (even overripe is fine) tomatoes for best results.

2 tablespoons extra-virgin olive oil

2 large onions, chopped

2 cloves garlic, minced

2 large celery stalks, peeled and diced

2 cups water

2 pounds ripe tomatoes, chopped

1 medium potato, scrubbed and finely diced

2 tablespoons chopped fresh dill

1 teaspoon salt-free seasoning
    (see page 4 for brands)

4 large ears fresh corn

½ cup Silk creamer

1½ to 2 cups salt-free tomato juice,
    as needed

1 tablespoon lemon juice, or to taste

Salt and freshly ground pepper to taste

Fresh herb or herbs of your choice (parsley,
    dill, oregano, etc.) for garnish

Per serving:
Calories: 200   Total fat: 9 g   Protein: 5 g   Fiber: 6 g
Carbohydrate: 33 g   Cholesterol: 0 mg   Sodium: 52 mg

Heat the oil in a soup pot. Add the onions, garlic, and celery and sauté over medium-low heat, stirring frequently, until all are golden. Add the water, tomatoes, and potato. Bring to a rapid simmer, then lower the heat. Cover and simmer gently until the potato is tender, about 15 to 20 minutes.

Add the dill and seasoning, and simmer for 5 minutes longer. Remove from the heat and allow to cool to room temperature.

Meanwhile, cook the corn until just tender, then drain and allow it to cool. When cool enough to handle, scrape the kernels off the cobs with a sharp knife. Combine the corn kernels with the creamer in a food processor and process until smoothly pureed. Place in a container and refrigerate until needed. Once the tomato mixture has cooled, puree it in batches in a food processor until smoothly pureed, then return to the soup pot. Or insert an immersion blender into the soup pot and process until well pureed.

Add enough tomato juice to give the soup a slightly thick consistency. Stir in the lemon juice and season with salt and pepper. Refrigerate until chilled. To serve, fill each serving bowl about three-quarters full with the tomato soup. Place a ladleful of the sweet corn sauce in the center of each bowl, and garnish each serving with a sprinkling of fresh herbs.

Cool Carrot Puree with Broccoli
and lots of fresh dill

6 to 8 servings

This cheerfully colored soup can be the centerpiece of a summer meal, served with crusty bread or sandwiches and a bountiful salad.

2 tablespoons olive oil

2 large onions, chopped

4 cups water with 2 vegetable bouillon cubes, or other stock option (page 9)

1 pound carrots, peeled and finely diced

1 large potato, peeled and finely diced

2 large ripe tomatoes, chopped

2 bay leaves

2 teaspoons salt-free seasoning (see page 4 for brands)

1 large broccoli crown, finely chopped

1½ cups rice milk, more or less as needed

¼ cup minced fresh dill, to taste, plus extra for garnish

Salt and freshly ground pepper to taste

Vegan Sour Cream (page 7) for garnish, optional

Per serving:
Calories: 172   Total fat: 6 g   Protein: 4 g   Fiber: 5 g
Carbohydrate: 28 g   Cholesterol: 0 mg   Sodium: 110 mg

Heat the oil in a soup pot. Add the onions and sauté over medium-low heat until golden.

Add the water with bouillon cubes, carrots, potato, and tomatoes. Stir in the bay leaves and seasoning. Bring to a rapid simmer, then lower the heat. Cover and simmer gently until the vegetables are tender, about 20 minutes. Allow the soup to cool to room temperature. Discard the bay leaves.

Transfer the solid ingredients to a food processor, in batches if necessary, and process until smoothly pureed. Return to the soup pot. Or insert an immersion blender into the pot and process until smoothly pureed.

Steam the broccoli in a large saucepan with about an inch of water until bright green and tender-crisp. Drain in a colander and rinse briefly with cool water. Stir the broccoli into the soup.

Add enough rice milk to give the soup a slightly thick consistency. Stir in the dill, then season with salt and pepper. Let the soup cool to room temperature, then refrigerate until chilled. Garnish each serving with a dollop of sour cream, if desired, and a sprinkling of dill.

Quick Cool Pinto Bean Puree

with tomatoes, peppers, and olives

6 servings

With the help of a food processor, this tasty, no-cook soup will be ready to eat in minutes. Serve with stone-ground tortilla chips or warmed flour tortillas.

Two 16-ounce cans pinto beans, drained
    and rinsed
One 16-ounce can salt-free stewed
    tomatoes, undrained
2 scallions, white and green parts, coarsely
    chopped, plus extra for garnish
¼ cup fresh cilantro or parsley leaves
Juice of 1 lemon
1 teaspoon chili powder
1 teaspoon ground cumin
1 medium green bell pepper, cut into
    1-inch pieces
4 ripe plum tomatoes, cut into large chunks
½ cup pitted black olives
¼ cup chopped mild green chilies (fresh
    or canned), optional
1½ cups water
Finely diced avocado for garnish, optional

Per serving:
Calories: 180   Total fat: 3 g   Protein: 10 g   Fiber: 10 g
Carbohydrate: 31 g   Cholesterol: 0 mg   Sodium: 465 mg

Combine the beans, canned tomatoes, scallions, and cilantro in a food processor and process until pureed, leaving just a bit of texture. Transfer to a large serving container and stir in the lemon juice, chili powder, and cumin.

Place the green pepper and fresh tomatoes in the food processor and pulse on and off 2 or 3 times. Add the olives and pulse on and off quickly, 2 or 3 times more, or until the vegetables are chopped into approximately ¼-inch pieces. Take care not to overprocess. Stir into the bean puree, then add the chilies, if desired.

Stir in the water, using more or less as needed to give the soup a medium-thick consistency. Serve at once or cover and refrigerate until needed. Garnish each serving with diced avocado, if desired, and additional scallions, thinly sliced.

Creamy Avocado Soup
with red bell pepper and fresh herbs

4 to 6 servings

A quick and easy no-cook soup, this is remark-
ably refreshing on a hot summer day. It's best
eaten on the same day as it is made, since
avocado discolors and does not keep well under
refrigeration once peeled. This soup makes a
great opener for a Southwestern-style meal of
burritos, enchiladas, or the like.

2 large ripe avocados, pitted and peeled
Juice of ½ lemon
1 recipe Vegan Sour Cream (page 7)
2 cups rice milk, more or less as needed
1 medium red bell pepper, finely chopped
2 scallions, green parts only, thinly sliced
2 tablespoons finely chopped fresh dill
2 tablespoons finely chopped fresh
    cilantro or parsley
1 teaspoon ground cumin
½ teaspoon good-quality curry powder
Salt and freshly ground pepper to taste

Per serving:
Calories: 326   Total fat: 24 g   Protein: 7 g   Fiber: 4 g
Carbohydrate: 26 g   Cholesterol: 0 mg   Sodium: 186 mg

Finely dice enough avocado to make 1 cup, then mash
the remainder well. Combine the diced and mashed
avocados in a serving container and mix immediately
with the lemon juice.

Stir in the sour cream, then enough rice milk to give the
soup a slightly thick consistency. Stir in the remaining
ingredients and refrigerate, covered, until thoroughly
chilled.

A first-rate soup is more creative than a
second-rate painting.

—Abraham Maslow (1908–1970)

Classic Gazpacho
A garden-fresh no-cook soup

6 servings

A collection of vegetarian soups wouldn't be complete without this Spanish classic. It's especially delicious topped with Garlic Croutons (page 159).

The base:
2 cups coarsely chopped ripe tomatoes
⅔ large cucumber, peeled and cut into chunks
⅔ large green or red bell pepper, cut into chunks
2 scallions, green parts only, cut into several pieces
Handful of parsley sprigs
1 to 2 tablespoons chopped fresh dill

To finish the soup:
3 cups salt-free tomato juice, or as needed
⅓ large cucumber, peeled and finely diced
⅓ large green or red bell pepper, finely diced
2 ripe tomatoes, finely diced
1 large carrot, peeled and finely diced
Juice of ½ to 1 lemon, to taste
2 teaspoons chili powder, or to taste
Dried hot red pepper flakes or hot sauce to taste, optional
Salt and freshly ground pepper to taste

Per serving:
Calories: 68   Total fat: 1 g   Protein: 3 g   Fiber: 4 g
Carbohydrate: 16 g   Cholesterol: 0 mg   Sodium: 35 mg

Place all the ingredients for the base in a food processor. Puree until fairly smooth.

Transfer the puree to a serving container. Stir in enough tomato juice to give the soup a slightly thick consistency.

Stir in the remaining ingredients, using red pepper flakes if you'd like a spicier soup. Cover and refrigerate for at least an hour before serving.

Zesty Green Gazpacho

Summery veggies enlivened by Southwestern seasonings

6 servings

A splendid no-cook soup that will awaken taste buds dulled by summer heat. This soup can be eaten as soon as it is made, but definitely benefits from having time to stand for several hours so that the lively flavors can mingle. This soup is a great first course for a Mexican or Southwestern-style meal.

2 large cucumbers, peeled, quartered
   lengthwise, and seeded

1 large green bell pepper

6 romaine or large curly green leaf lettuce
   leaves, coarsely chopped

2 scallions, white and green parts, coarsely
   chopped

⅓ cup fresh cilantro leaves

½ cup store-bought salsa verde
   (tomatillo sauce)

1 mild or hot fresh green chili pepper,
   seeded and minced

Juice of 1 lime

1 teaspoon ground cumin

1 recipe Vegan Sour Cream (page 7)

1 to 2 cups rice milk, as needed

Salt and freshly ground pepper to taste

Per serving:
Calories: 100   Total fat: 2 g   Protein: 5 g   Fiber: 3 g
Carbohydrate: 17 g   Cholesterol: 0 mg   Sodium: 200 mg

Finely chop about half of one cucumber and half of the bell pepper and set aside. Coarsely chop the rest and place in a food processor along with the lettuce, scallions, and cilantro. Process until pureed, with a little texture remaining. Transfer to a large serving container.

Stir in the reserved cucumber and bell pepper, followed by the salsa verde, chili pepper, lime juice, cumin, sour cream, and 1 cup rice milk. Stir well to combine. Add more rice milk as needed to give the soup a slightly thick consistency.

Season with salt and pepper. Serve at once, or cover and refrigerate for an hour or so, until thoroughly chilled.

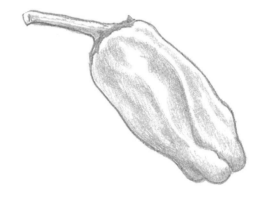

Spiced Summer Fruit Soup

Berries, plums, peaches, and grapes in a wine-scented base

6 or more servings

This and the following berry soup are the only fruit soups in this chapter that need a bit of cooking. The wine and spices give it a wonderfully complex flavor.

1 cup fresh blueberries

3 sweet red plums, diced

4 medium ripe peaches, diced

1 cup seedless red or green grapes

1 cup hulled and chopped strawberries

Juice of ½ lemon

4½ cups apple juice

One 2-inch stick cinnamon

5 whole cloves

⅓ cup semisweet red wine

3 tablespoons natural granulated sugar or
    agave nectar, or to taste

Per serving:
Calories: 212   Total fat: 1 g   Protein: 1 g   Fiber: 4 g
Carbohydrate: 50 g   Cholesterol: 0 mg   Sodium: 10 mg

Combine all the ingredients in a soup pot. Bring to a rapid simmer, then lower the heat. Cover and simmer gently for 20 to 25 minutes, until the fruit is tender.

Allow the soup to cool, then refrigerate until chilled. If too dense, adjust the consistency with more apple juice.

---

*He that would have the fruit
must climb the tree.*

—Thomas Fuller
    Gnomologia, 1732

Chilled Berry Soup

A medley of blueberries, strawberries, and raspberries

6 servings

Enjoy the convergence of strawberries and mid-summer berries in a sweetly spiced broth.

1 pint blueberries

1 pint strawberries, hulled and
    coarsely chopped

1 cup raspberries

2 medium peaches or nectarines, chopped

4 cups raspberry or strawberry juice

⅓ cup dry red or white wine

Juice of ½ lemon

1 teaspoon cinnamon

½ teaspoon ground allspice

¼ teaspoon ground nutmeg

Natural granulated sugar, maple syrup,
    or agave nectar to taste, if needed

Sliced strawberries for garnish

Per serving:
Calories: 162   Total fat: 1 g   Protein: 2 g   Fiber: 6 g
Carbohydrate: 38 g   Cholesterol: 0 mg   Sodium: 9 mg

Combine all the ingredients except the last two in a soup pot. Bring to a rapid simmer, then lower the heat. Cover and simmer gently for 10 to 15 minutes, or until the fruit is tender. Remove from the heat.

Taste the soup, and if you'd like it sweeter, add sweetener of your choice—depending on the sweetness of the fruit and the fruit juice, you may not need to add sweetener at all, or very little.

Allow the soup to cool to room temperature, then refrigerate until thoroughly chilled. Garnish each serving with a few strawberry slices.

Strawberry Colada Soup

A celebration of strawberries in creamy coconut milk

6 servings

This super-quick no-cook soup is delicious enough to serve as a dessert.

1½ cups organic strawberry juice

One 13.5-ounce can light coconut milk

1 quart ripe strawberries, hulled and cut into
    approximately ½-inch chunks

2 to 3 tablespoons natural granulated sugar
    or agave nectar, or to taste

¼ teaspoon cinnamon

Fresh mint leaves for garnish, optional

Per serving:
Calories: 113   Total fat: 4 g   Protein: 1 g   Fiber: 3 g
Carbohydrate: 21 g   Cholesterol: 0 mg   Sodium: 8 mg

Combine the strawberry juice and coconut milk in a serving container and whisk together.

Crush a scant cup of the strawberries, then stir into the juice–coconut milk mixture, followed by the cut strawberries.

Sweeten as desired, then whisk in the cinnamon. Refrigerate for an hour or so before serving. If desired, garnish each serving with a few mint leaves.

Chilled Cantaloupe Soup
enhanced with the flavors of mango and lime

6 servings

It takes minutes to make this sweet soup. Try serving it after a meal rather than before—it's a wonderful palate cooler after a spicy meal. Or it can be the main event at lunch on a hot summer day, served with blueberry muffins.

8 heaping cups lush, ripe cantaloupe,
   cut into 2-inch chunks
1½ cups mango nectar or
   orange-mango juice
1 tablespoon lime juice
2 to 3 tablespoons agave nectar or maple
   syrup, to taste
Pinch of cinnamon
Pinch of ground nutmeg
1 cup berries, any variety, for garnish
Fresh mint leaves for garnish, optional

Per serving:
Calories: 148   Total fat: 1 g   Protein: 2 g   Fiber: 3 g
Carbohydrate: 37 g   Cholesterol: 0 mg   Sodium: 24 mg

Set aside about 2 cups of the melon chunks and place the rest in a food processor or blender. Process until smoothly pureed, then add the juices, nectar, and spices. Process again until thoroughly blended. Transfer the mixture to a serving container.

Cut the reserved melon chunks into ½-inch dice and stir them into the soup. Cover and chill for an hour or so before serving. Garnish each serving with some berries and 2 or 3 mint leaves, if desired.

Melon Medley

A trio of melons in a creamy citrus base

6 servings

A perfect dessert soup to make in July, when melons are at their sweetest. This makes a refreshing finish to a grilled meal.

3 cups watermelon, cut into ½-inch dice
  and seeded
3 cups honeydew melon, cut into ½-inch dice
1 medium cantaloupe, very ripe, seeded and
  cut into large chunks
1 pint vanilla or lemon nondairy ice cream
2 cups orange juice, preferably fresh
Blueberries for garnish
Fresh mint leaves for garnish

Per serving:
Calories: 223   Total fat: 5 g   Protein: 3 g   Fiber: 2 g
Carbohydrate: 43 g   Cholesterol: 0 mg   Sodium: 120 mg

Friends are like melons,
Shall I tell you why?
To find one good
You must a hundred try.

—Claude Mermet, 1600

To make part of this soup ahead of time, prepare the watermelon and honeydew as directed, combine in a mixing bowl, then cover and refrigerate. Place the cantaloupe chunks in a separate container. Cover and chill for an hour or more.

Just before serving, combine the cantaloupe, nondairy ice cream, and orange juice in a food processor and process, in batches if necessary, until smoothly pureed.

Divide among 6 serving bowls. Place approximately 1 cup of the watermelon and honeydew mixture in each. Scatter some blueberries over the top of each serving and garnish with 2 or 3 mint leaves.

Minted Peach Soup
Creamy and juicy, with a hint of ginger

6 servings

For success with this soup, don't settle for less than luscious, tree-ripened peaches. Avoid peaches that are bought rock-hard, only to ripen to flavorless mush after several days of waiting.

2½ pounds ripe, juicy peaches, pitted

2 cups peach, pear, or mango nectar

½ cup rice milk

½ cup Silk creamer

1 teaspoon vanilla extract

½ teaspoon grated fresh ginger

Dash of ground nutmeg

2 tablespoons crushed fresh mint leaves or
 1 mint tea bag

1 to 2 tablespoons maple syrup or agave
 nectar, or to taste

Per serving:
Calories: 163   Total fat: 3 g   Protein: 2 g   Fiber: 4 g
Carbohydrate: 37 g   Cholesterol: 0 mg   Sodium: 27 mg

A little peach in an orchard grew,—
A little peach of emerald hue;
Warmed by the sun and wet by the
  dew,
It grew.

—Eugene Field
  "The Little Peach," 1889

Dice about 2 cups of the peaches and set aside. Place the rest in a food processor with the nectar. Process until smoothly pureed, then transfer to a serving container.

Stir in the rice milk, creamer, vanilla, and spices.

In a cup, steep the fresh mint leaves or mint tea in about ½ cup boiling water for 10 to 15 minutes. Remove the leaves or tea bag and stir the infusion into the serving container.

Stir in the reserved peaches and add syrup to taste. Refrigerate for an hour or two to allow the flavors to blend. Before serving, stir the soup and adjust the consistency with more nectar if too dense.

Vanilla Fruit Cup Soup

A colorful fruit salad transformed into a dessert soup

6 servings

Requiring no cooking and no blending, this soup takes full advantage of the lush fruits of midsummer.

2 cups berries, as desired (blueberries, raspberries, or chopped strawberries, or a combination)

½ medium cantaloupe, cut into ½-inch dice

2 cups seeded watermelon, cut into ½-inch dice

1½ cups seedless green grapes, left whole if small or halved if large

2 peaches or nectarines, cut into ½-inch dice

2 cups lemon or vanilla soy yogurt

1 teaspoon vanilla extract

1½ cups white grape juice, more or less as needed

1 to 2 tablespoons agave nectar or maple syrup, optional

Per serving:
Calories: 215   Total fat: 2 g   Protein: 4 g   Fiber: 3 g
Carbohydrate: 47 g   Cholesterol: 0 mg   Sodium: 23 mg

Combine all the ingredients except the last two in a serving container.

Add enough juice to give the soup a slightly thick consistency. Taste, and if you want extra sweetness, add nectar to your liking. Cover and chill for an hour or two before serving.

Fruit, as it was our primitive and most excellent as well as most innocent food, whilst it grew in Paradise ... so it has still preserved, and retained no small tincture of its original and celestial virtue.

—John Evelyn
   Complete Gard'ner, 1693

ACCOMPANIMENTS

Here is a selection of quick breads,
muffins, scones, and such to accompany
your soups. Simple to prepare, these can
be made while the soup is simmering,
then served fresh and warm.

Quick Sunflower-Cheese Bread

Makes 1 loaf, about 12 slices

This tasty bread goes well with many soups. Try it with mixed vegetable, tomato-based, and bean soups.

2 cups whole wheat pastry flour

1½ teaspoons baking powder

1 teaspoon baking soda

½ teaspoon salt

1 cup plain soy yogurt

2 tablespoons safflower oil

1 tablespoon maple syrup or agave nectar

1 teaspoon prepared mustard

¼ cup rice milk, or more as needed

1 cup firmly packed grated cheddar-style
   nondairy cheese

¼ cup toasted sunflower seeds

Per slice (12 slices per loaf):
Calories: 157   Total fat: 7 g   Protein: 4 g   Fiber: 4 g
Carbohydrate: 21 g   Cholesterol: 0 mg   Sodium: 325 mg

Preheat the oven to 350 degrees.

Combine the first 4 (dry) ingredients in a mixing bowl and stir together.

In another bowl, combine the yogurt, oil, syrup, mustard, and rice milk. Whisk together until well blended. Make a well in the dry ingredients and pour in the wet mixture. Stir until well combined, adding more rice milk as needed to make a smooth, slightly stiff batter.

Fold in the cheese and half of the sunflower seeds.

Pour the batter into a lightly oiled 9-by-5-by-3-inch loaf pan. Sprinkle the remaining sunflower seeds over the top.

Bake for 45 minutes, or until the top is golden brown and crusty. When the loaf pan is cool enough to handle, remove the loaf, place it on a rack, and allow it to cool somewhat before slicing.

Green Chili Cornbread

Makes 12 squares

This moist cornbread is an ideal companion to bean soups and chilis.

1½ cups stone-ground whole-grain cornmeal
½ cup unbleached white flour
¼ cup toasted wheat germ
1 teaspoon baking soda
½ teaspoon baking powder
1 teaspoon salt
1 cup plain soy yogurt
2 tablespoons olive oil
¼ cup rice milk, or more as needed
1 small fresh hot chili, seeded and minced,
    or one 4-ounce can chopped
    mild green chilies
½ cup frozen corn kernels, thawed

Per square (12 squares per pan):
Calories: 128   Total fat: 4 g   Protein: 3 g   Fiber: 2 g
Carbohydrate: 22 g   Cholesterol: 0 mg   Sodium: 257 mg

Preheat the oven to 400 degrees.

Combine the first 6 (dry) ingredients in a mixing bowl and stir together.

Make a well in the center of the dry ingredients. Pour in the yogurt, oil, and rice milk. Stir until well combined, adding more rice milk as needed to make a smooth, slightly stiff batter.

Stir in the chili and corn kernels. Pour the mixture into an oiled 9-inch-square baking pan. Bake for 20 to 25 minutes, or until the top is golden and a knife inserted in the center tests clean. Let cool slightly; cut into squares and serve warm.

Pray let me, an American, inform the gentleman, who seems ignorant of the matter, that Indian corn, take it all in all, is one of the most agreeable and wholesome grains in the world.

—Benjamin Franklin (1706–1790)

Hearty Bean Bread

Makes 12 squares

Try serving this offbeat pan bread, studded with pink beans and scallions, with hearty vegetable soups and stews. I especially like this with soups that feature corn and/or squash.

1½ cups whole wheat pastry flour

½ cup cornmeal

1 teaspoon baking soda

1 teaspoon baking powder

1 teaspoon salt

½ teaspoon ground cumin

1 tablespoon natural granulated sugar

1 cup plain soy yogurt

2 tablespoons olive oil

¼ cup rice milk, or more as needed

1 cup canned pink or pinto beans, drained
    and rinsed

3 scallions, green parts only, thinly sliced

Per square (12 squares per pan):
Calories: 132   Total fat: 3 g   Protein: 4 g   Fiber: 4 g
Carbohydrate: 23 g   Cholesterol: 0 mg   Sodium: 379 mg

Preheat the oven to 375 degrees.

Combine the first 7 (dry) ingredients in a mixing bowl and stir together.

Make a well in the center of the dry ingredients. Pour in the yogurt, oil, and rice milk. Stir until well combined, adding more rice milk as needed to make a smooth, slightly stiff batter. Gently stir in the beans and scallions.

Pour the mixture into an oiled 9-inch-square baking pan. Bake for 20 to 25 minutes, or until the top is golden and a knife inserted in the center tests clean. Let cool slightly; cut into squares and serve warm.

Tomato-Olive Bread

Makes 1 loaf, about 12 slices

Here's an unusual bread that teams beautifully with many kinds of soup. Try this with anything from hearty bean soups to light, brothy ones. Use your favorite kind of olive; it works well with most any variety.

2¼ cups whole wheat pastry flour

¼ cup wheat germ

2 teaspoons baking powder

½ teaspoon salt

1 tablespoon natural granulated sugar

½ teaspoon ground cumin

¼ teaspoon dried basil

Pinch of dried thyme

1 cup rice milk, or more as needed

2 tablespoons olive oil

1½ cups finely chopped ripe tomato

½ cup finely chopped pitted olives,
   any variety

Per slice (12 slices per loaf):
Calories: 130   Total fat: 4 g   Protein: 4 g   Fiber: 3 g
Carbohydrate: 22 g   Cholesterol: 0 mg   Sodium: 218 mg

Preheat the oven to 350 degrees.

Combine the first 8 (dry) ingredients in a mixing bowl and stir together. Make a well in the center and add the rice milk and oil. Stir until well combined, adding more rice milk as needed to make a smooth, slightly stiff batter.

Fold in the tomato and olives. Pour the batter into a lightly oiled 9-by-5-by-3-inch loaf pan. Bake for 45 to 50 minutes, or until a knife inserted into the center of the loaf tests clean. Let cool until just warm, then cut into slices to serve.

Except the vine, there is no plant which bears a fruit of as great an importance as the olive.

—Pliny the Elder
   Historia Naturalis, 79 B.C.

Focaccia Bread

Makes 1 round loaf, about 8 wedges

Although this excellent traditional Italian bread is yeasted, it does not take as long to make as other yeasted breads, since it requires only one rather brief rising. If you are making a long-simmering soup, this bread will likely fit into the time frame. It's a natural pairing with Italian-style soups such as Minestrone (page 50), but it's good with most any tomato-based soup.

1 package active dry yeast
1 cup warm water
1 tablespoon natural granulated sugar
¼ cup extra-virgin olive oil
1½ cups whole wheat flour
1 cup unbleached white flour
1 teaspoon salt
1 tablespoon minced fresh garlic
Coarse salt
Dried oregano or rosemary

Per wedge (8 wedges per loaf):
Calories: 206   Total fat: 7 g   Protein: 5 g   Fiber: 3 g
Carbohydrate: 31 g   Cholesterol: 0 mg   Sodium: 294 mg

Pour the yeast into the warm water and let stand to dissolve for 5 to 10 minutes. Stir in the sugar and 2 tablespoons of the oil.

Combine the flours and salt in a large mixing bowl. Work the yeast mixture in using your hands, then turn out onto a well-floured board. Knead for 5 minutes, adding additional flour if the dough is too sticky. Shape into a round and roll out into a circle with a 12-inch diameter.

Place on an oiled and floured baking sheet, cover with a tea towel, and let rise in a warm place for 30 to 40 minutes.

Preheat the oven to 400 degrees.

When the dough has finished rising, poke shallow holes into its surface with your fingers, at even intervals. Sprinkle the remaining 2 tablespoons of olive oil over the top evenly, followed by the garlic, coarse salt, and herb.

Bake for 20 to 25 minutes, or until the bread is golden on top and sounds hollow when tapped. Serve warm, cut into wedges, or just have everyone break off pieces.

Bread made from pure wheat flour ... finely moulded and baked, comforteth and strengtheneth the heart, and maketh a man fat, and preserveth health.

—William Vaughn
Directions for Health, 1600

Whole Wheat Vegetable Muffins

Makes 1 dozen

Tiny bits of fresh vegetables give these muffins a fascinating flavor and texture. These are particularly good with pureed soups, as well as those that focus on one primary ingredient such as carrots or squash.

1 cup assorted fresh vegetables, cut into 1-inch chunks (choose from among carrot, green or red bell pepper, radish, peeled broccoli stem, and zucchini)
2 cups whole wheat pastry flour
2 tablespoons wheat germ or ground flaxseeds
1½ teaspoons baking powder
½ teaspoon salt
¾ cup plain soy yogurt
2 tablespoons olive oil
1 tablespoon maple syrup or agave nectar
¼ cup rice milk, or more as needed
Poppy seeds for topping, optional

Per muffin:
Calories: 115   Total fat: 3 g   Protein: 4 g   Fiber: 3 g
Carbohydrate: 20 g   Cholesterol: 0 mg   Sodium: 150 mg

Preheat the oven to 350 degrees.

Place the vegetable chunks in a food processor. Pulse on and off until the vegetables are finely minced; take care not to overprocess. Set aside.

Combine the next 4 (dry) ingredients in a mixing bowl and stir together. Make a well in the center. Pour in the yogurt, oil, syrup, and rice milk. Stir until well combined, adding more rice milk as needed to make a smooth, slightly stiff batter. Stir in the vegetables.

Divide the batter among 12 lightly oiled or paper-lined muffin tins. Top with the optional poppy seeds. Bake for 20 to 25 minutes, or until the tops are golden brown. Remove the muffins from the tins as soon as they are cool enough to handle, and cool them on a rack or a plate.

Variation:

Add ¼ cup minced dried tomato, reconstituted or oil-cured, as preferred.

Five muffins are enough for any man at a meal.

—E.V. Knox
Gorgeous Times, 1928

Cheese and Herb Corn Muffins

Makes 1 dozen

Moist and flavorful, these muffins pair nicely with bean soups. Try them with Long-Simmering Black Bean Soup (page 38).

1 cup stone-ground whole-grain cornmeal

1½ cups whole wheat pastry flour

1 teaspoon baking powder

½ teaspoon baking soda

½ teaspoon salt

1 cup plain soy yogurt

3 tablespoons olive oil

¼ cup rice milk, or more as needed

1 cup grated cheddar-style nondairy cheese

½ cup cooked fresh or thawed frozen
    corn kernels

3 tablespoons mixed fresh herbs, minced
    (choose from among oregano, thyme,
    tarragon, and chives)

Per muffin:
Calories: 172   Total fat: 7 g   Protein: 4 g   Fiber: 4 g
Carbohydrate: 25 g   Cholesterol: 0 mg   Sodium: 160 mg

*Her hair that lay along her back
Was yellow like ripe corn.*

—Dante Gabriel Rossetti
    "The Blessed Damozel," 1847

Preheat the oven to 400 degrees.

Combine the first 5 (dry) ingredients in a mixing bowl and stir together. Make a well in the center and pour in the yogurt, oil, and rice milk. Stir until well combined, adding more rice milk as needed to make a smooth, slightly stiff batter.

Fold in the grated cheese, corn kernels, and herbs.

Divide the batter among 12 lightly oiled or paper-lined muffin tins. Bake for 20 to 25 minutes, or until the tops are golden brown and a toothpick inserted into the center of one tests clean.

Cool on a rack, then store in an airtight container as soon as the muffins are at room temperature.

Oat-Walnut Muffins

Makes 1 dozen

Tender and just slightly sweet, these are good teamed with spicy or chunky soups and stews.

1¼ cups whole wheat flour

¾ cup rolled oats

1½ teaspoons baking powder

½ teaspoon baking soda

½ teaspoon salt

1 cup unsweetened applesauce

2 tablespoons safflower oil

¼ cup rice milk, or more as needed

½ cup chopped walnuts

Per muffin:

Calories: 125   Total fat: 6 g   Protein: 3 g   Fiber: 3 g
Carbohydrate: 16 g   Cholesterol: 0 mg   Sodium: 100 mg

Preheat the oven to 350 degrees.

Combine the first 5 (dry) ingredients in a mixing bowl and stir together. Make a well in the center and pour in the applesauce, oil, and rice milk. Stir until well combined, adding more rice milk as needed to make a smooth, slightly stiff batter.

Fold in the walnuts, then divide the batter among 12 lightly oiled or paper-lined muffin tins. Bake for 20 to 25 minutes, or until the tops are golden and a toothpick inserted into the center of one tests clean.

Cool on a rack, then store in an airtight container as soon as the muffins are at room temperature.

Barley or Rice Triangles

Makes about 20

These offbeat little griddle biscuits pair well with bean soups, purees, and soups that feature root vegetables.

1¼ cups whole wheat pastry flour

¼ cup stone-ground whole-grain cornmeal

1 teaspoon baking powder

1 teaspoon salt

3 tablespoons nonhydrogenated
    margarine, softened

1 cup well-cooked barley or brown rice

¼ cup rice milk, or as needed

Per biscuit:
Calories: 55   Total fat: 2 g   Protein: 1 g   Fiber: 1 g
Carbohydrate: 9 g   Cholesterol: 0 mg   Sodium: 150 mg

Combine the first 4 (dry) ingredients in a mixing bowl and stir together. Work the margarine into the flour mixture with the tines of a fork or a pastry blender until the mixture resembles coarse crumbs.

Stir in the cooked grain, then add enough rice milk to hold the mixture together as a firm dough, working it together with your hands.

Divide the dough into 2 parts. On a well-floured board, roll out one part until it is ¼ inch thick. With a sharp knife, cut the dough into triangular pieces with approximately 2-inch sides. Repeat with the remaining dough; gather up any dough left over from cutting and roll out again until it is all used up.

Heat a griddle or large nonstick skillet that has been sprayed with cooking oil spray. Cook the triangles over medium heat until they are touched with light brown on both sides. Transfer to a plate to cool, and once the triangles are at room temperature, store them in an airtight container.

Cheddar-Oat Griddle Biscuits

Makes about 20

These little biscuits pair especially well with mild-flavored soups featuring cauliflower or broccoli, but they are compatible with most any kind of vegetable soup.

1 cup whole wheat pastry flour

1 cup rolled oats

1 teaspoon salt

1 teaspoon baking powder

3 tablespoons nonhydrogenated
     margarine, softened

1 cup grated cheddar-style nondairy cheese

¼ cup rice milk, or as needed

Per biscuit:
Calories: 68   Total fat: 4 g   Protein: 2 g   Fiber: 2 g
Carbohydrate: 8 g   Cholesterol: 0 mg   Sodium: 190 mg

Combine the first 4 (dry) ingredients in a mixing bowl and stir together. Work the margarine into the flour mixture with the tines of a fork or a pastry blender until the mixture resembles coarse crumbs. Stir in the cheese, then add enough rice milk to hold the mixture together as a firm dough, working it together with your hands.

Turn out onto a well-floured board and roll the dough out to a ¼-inch thickness. Cut the dough into 2-inch rounds with a cookie cutter or the rim of a glass. Gather up leftover dough, roll out, and cut until all the dough has been used up.

Heat a griddle or large nonstick skillet that has been sprayed with cooking oil spray. Cook the biscuits on both sides over medium heat until golden brown. Cool on a plate, then transfer to an airtight container when cooled to room temperature.

Potato-Rye Griddle Biscuits

Makes 16 to 18

These are especially good with soups containing beets, cabbage, or strong greens.

1 cup rye flour

¾ cup unbleached white flour

2 tablespoons ground flaxseeds

1 teaspoon baking powder

1 teaspoon salt

1 teaspoon caraway seeds, optional

1 cup well-mashed cooked potato

¼ cup rice milk, or as needed

3 tablespoons olive oil

Per biscuit:
Calories: 77   Total fat: 3 g   Protein: 2 g   Fiber: 1 g
Carbohydrate: 11 g   Cholesterol: 0 mg   Sodium: 160 mg

Combine the first 5 (dry) ingredients plus the optional caraway seeds in a mixing bowl and stir together. Make a well in the center and add the mashed potato, rice milk, and oil. Work together, first with a spoon and then with your hands, adding just enough rice milk to form a smooth, soft dough. Add just a bit more flour if the dough seems too sticky to handle.

Divide the dough into 3 or 4 parts and roll each out to ¼-inch thickness on a floured board. Cut the dough into 2-inch rounds with a cookie cutter or the rim of a glass. Knead together the leftover dough, roll out, and cut until all the dough has been used up.

Heat a griddle or large nonstick skillet that has been sprayed with cooking oil spray. Cook each round over medium heat for 5 to 7 minutes on each side, or until golden. Serve warm.

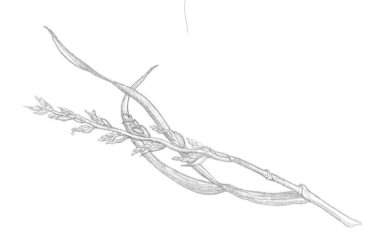

Onion-Rye Scones

Makes 8

Moist and slightly crumbly, these scones team especially well with soups made of root vegetables—potatoes, parsnips, and the like.

1½ cups rye flour
¾ cup whole wheat pastry flour
2 teaspoons baking powder
1 teaspoon salt
3 tablespoons nonhydrogenated
  margarine, softened
2 tablespoons molasses or maple syrup
¼ cup rice milk, or as needed

Topping:
2 teaspoons olive oil
1 medium onion, quartered and thinly sliced
Poppy seeds

Per scone:
Calories: 172   Total fat: 5 g   Protein: 4 g   Fiber: 4 g
Carbohydrate: 29 g   Cholesterol: 0 mg   Sodium: 600 mg

Preheat the oven to 350 degrees.

Combine the first 4 (dry) ingredients in a mixing bowl and stir together. Work the margarine into the flour mixture with a pastry blender or the tines of a fork until the mixture resembles a coarse meal.

In a small bowl, whisk the molasses together with the rice milk. Work into the flour mixture, adding enough rice milk to form a soft dough. If the dough is sticky, work in some additional flour.

Transfer the dough to a well-floured board and knead briefly with floured hands.

Form the dough into a ball, then roll into a round 9 inches in diameter and place on a lightly oiled baking sheet. Score the round with a knife, about halfway through the dough, into 8 equal wedges.

For the topping, heat the oil in a small skillet. Add the onion and sauté over medium heat until lightly browned. Distribute the onion evenly over the scones, then lightly press them down with a spatula. Sprinkle with poppy seeds.

Bake for 15 to 20 minutes, or until the tops are golden. Let cool somewhat before slicing.

Currant Griddle Scones

Makes 8

If you'd like an accompaniment to summer fruit soups but don't want to turn on the oven, these slightly sweet scones are just the thing to make.

1½ cups whole wheat pastry flour

1½ teaspoons baking powder

¼ teaspoon cinnamon

¼ cup natural granulated sugar

¼ cup nonhydrogenated margarine, softened

¼ cup rice milk, or as needed

⅔ cup dried currants

¼ cup finely chopped walnuts

Per scone:
Calories: 204   Total fat: 7 g   Protein: 4 g   Fiber: 7 g
Carbohydrate: 33 g   Cholesterol: 0 mg   Sodium: 120 mg

I stamp this kiss
Upon thy currant lip.

—William Shakespeare
The Two Noble Kinsmen, c. 1634

Combine the first 4 (dry) ingredients in a mixing bowl and stir together. Work the margarine into the flour mixture with a pastry blender or the tines of a fork until the mixture resembles coarse crumbs.

Add enough rice milk to hold the dough together, working it together with your hands. Work the currants and walnuts in with your hands, then turn the dough out onto a well-floured board and knead briefly.

Form the dough into a ball, then roll out to a thickness of about ¼ inch. Cut the dough into 2-inch rounds with a cookie cutter or the rim of a glass. Gather up any leftover dough, roll out, and cut until all the dough has been used up.

Heat a griddle or large nonstick skillet that has been sprayed with cooking oil spray. Cook the scones over medium heat or until golden brown on both sides. Cool on a rack and serve warm.

Scallion Pancakes

Makes about 24

These delectable little pancakes are appreciated by adults and children alike, and are the perfect accompaniment to Asian-style soups.

2 cups spelt flour or whole wheat pastry flour

1 teaspoon salt

½ teaspoon baking powder

2 tablespoons sesame seeds, optional

2 cups water

2 cups thinly sliced scallions, white and green parts

3 tablespoons olive oil, or as needed

Per pancake:
Calories: 50   Total fat: 2 g   Protein: 1 g   Fiber: 2 g
Carbohydrate: 9 g   Cholesterol: 0 mg   Sodium: 105 mg

Combine the first 3 (dry) ingredients plus the optional sesame seeds in a large mixing bowl and stir together.

Make a well in the center of the flour mixture and pour in the water. Whisk together until smooth, then stir in the scallions.

Heat enough oil to lightly coat a nonstick griddle or wide skillet. Ladle a scant ¼ cup batter onto the pan for each pancake. Cook over medium heat on both sides until golden brown. Remove to a paper towel–lined plate and keep warm (or start eating!) while cooking the remaining pancakes.

Chapatis

Makes 12

These simple, traditional Indian flatbreads are wonderful served with any of the curried soup and stew recipes in these pages.

2 cups whole wheat pastry flour
½ teaspoon salt
¾ cup water, or as needed

Per chapati:
Calories: 68   Total fat: 1 g   Protein: 3 g   Fiber: 2 g
Carbohydrate: 15 g   Cholesterol: 0 mg   Sodium: 95 mg

Combine the flour and salt in a mixing bowl and stir together. Add water a bit at a time until the dough holds together. Turn out onto a floured board and knead for about 5 minutes, or until smooth and elastic. Place the dough in a small floured bowl and cover with a clean tea towel. Let the dough rest for 30 minutes.

Divide the dough into 12 equal pieces and shape each into a ball.

Heat a small nonstick skillet coated with cooking oil spray.

Roll out each ball of dough into a thin round, about 5 inches in diameter. Cook one at a time on the skillet over medium heat until touched with light brown spots, about 3 to 4 minutes. Flip and cook on the other side; repeat with the other balls of dough. Keep the chapatis warm, stacked one atop another in foil, until all are done. Serve at once.

A Trio of Simple Accompaniments

Bruschetta: This Italian recipe for broad, garlicky toasts is a great all-purpose accompaniment for most any type of soup (except for fruit soups). Cut as many ¾-inch-thick slices as you need from a round of Italian bread. If it is whole-grain, so much the better. Place the slices on a nonstick baking sheet and bake in a preheated 350-degree oven for 10 to 15 minutes, turning once, or until both sides are golden and crisp. Or you may place them right on the oven rack, in which case they need not be turned. Watch them carefully!

Remove the toasts from the oven. When cool enough to handle, rub one side of each toast with the open side of a clove of garlic that has been cut in half lengthwise. If desired, brush a bit of olive oil on one side of the toasts as well.

Garlic Croutons: This idea is so simple that it scarcely qualifies as a recipe, yet few embellishments for soup are as simple and pleasing as this one. Making croutons is also a good way to use up bread that may otherwise go stale. Use ends and pieces of whole-grain bread, allowing about 1 small slice per serving. Rub each piece of bread gently on one or both sides with the open side of a garlic clove that has been cut in half lengthwise. Cut the bread into approximately ½-inch dice.

Prepare the croutons in one of the two following ways: Arrange on a baking sheet and bake in a 275-degree oven for 20 minutes or so, until dry and crisp. Or if the weather is warm and you don't wish to use the oven, simply toast the croutons in a heavy skillet over medium heat, stirring frequently, about 20 minutes, or until dry and crisp. Allow the croutons to cool on a plate. They may be used as soon as they have cooled, but if you can leave them out at room temperature for at least 30 minutes or so, they'll stay crisper in soup.

Frizzled Tortilla Strips: Curly fried corn tortilla strips are a fun topping for Southwestern-style soups and stews. Try these on Potato, Cheese, and Green Chili Soup (page 22), White Bean and Hominy Chili (page 68), or Zesty Green Gazpacho (page 134).

Cut corn tortillas into ½-inch by approximately 2-inch strips, allowing one tortilla per serving. Heat about ½ inch of olive oil in a deep skillet. Scatter the tortillas around the skillet so that there is just one layer frying at a time. Fry for 3 to 4 minutes or until crisp, then scoop out with a slotted spoon and continue cooking until you have as much as you need. Drain each batch on two layers of paper towels.

INDEX